F. W. L Thomas

Traditions of the Morrisons

F. W. L Thomas

Traditions of the Morrisons

ISBN/EAN: 9783337389420

Printed in Europe, USA, Canada, Australia, Japan

Cover: Foto ©ninafisch / pixelio.de

More available books at **www.hansebooks.com**

PROCEEDINGS OF THE SOCIETY

OF ANTIQUARIES OF SCOTLAND

Vol. XII

(1876 – 1878)

PP.
503 - 556

for private circulation, 1877.

"The Towneley Manuscripts: English Jacobite Ballads, Songs, and Satires." 4to. Printed for private circulation, 1877.

(15.) By Francis Compton Price, Esq.

"Facsimiles of Examples from the Press of William Caxton at Westminster." Privately printed. London, 1877. Small folio.

(16.) By Dr Batty Tuke, F.S.A. Scot.

Volume of Tracts relating to the Civil War, 1640-1660.

I.

TRADITIONS OF THE MORRISONS (CLAN MAC GHILLEMHUIRE), HEREDITARY JUDGES OF LEWIS. By Capt. F. W. L. Thomas, R.N., Vice-President S.A. Scot.

A letter communicated to the *Athenæum*, in March 1866, contained some account of the Lewis Clans founded on oral tradition. Since then I have collected much additional information concerning them, either from printed books and MSS., or from notices supplied to me by residents on the island.

In the letter to the *Athenæum* it was stated, on the authority of those around me, that time out of mind Lewis had been inhabited by three confederated clans—the Macleods, the Morrisons,[1] and the Macaulays. This statement is confirmed in a "Description of the Lewis, by John Morisone,[2] indweller there," which is inferred to have been written between 1678 and 1688. The "Indweller" states:—"The first and most ancient inhabitants of this countrie were three men of three several reaces, viz., Mores, the sone of Kennanus, whom the Irish historians call Makurich, whom they make to be naturall son to one of the kings of Norovay, some of whose posteritie remains in the land to this day. All the Morrisons in Scotland may challenge their descent from this man. The second was Iskair Mac Aulay, an Irishman, whose posteritie remain likewise to this day in the Lews. The third was Macnaicle, whose only daughter, Torquile, the first of that name (and sone to Claudius the son of Olipheus, who likewise is said to be the King of Norvay his sone), did violently espouse, and cut off immediately the whole race of Maknaicle, and possessed himself of the whole Lews, and continueth in his posteritie (Macleod Lews), during thirteen or fourteen generations, and so extinct before, or at least about 1600."[3]

[1] R. Chambers has, under the heading of "Family Characteristics," in his "Popular Rhymes of Scotland,"—"The Manly Morrisons. This is, or was, especially applicable to a family which had been settled for a long period at Woodend, in the parish of Kirkmichael, in Dumfriesshire, and become remarkable for the handsomeness of its cadets" (Collected Works, vol. vii. p. 97). It is still applicable to the Morrisons of the Outer Hebrides.

[2] From internal evidence it can be proved that the "Description" was written after 1678, and probably before 1688. He speaks of the destruction of Stornoway Castle, which took place in 1654, as having "lately" occurred. The writer was intimately acquainted with Lewis; when young, there were only three people in Lewis who knew the alphabet, but when he wrote, the head of the family at least was usually able to read and write. The author was probably the Rev. John Morrison, sometime minister of Urray, son of John Morrison of Bragar, and father of the Rev. John Morrison, minister of Petty.

[3] Spot. Mis. vol. ii. p. 341.

Such was the tradition of the origin of the ruling families in the seventeenth century, and it is first to be noted that the writer uses "Irish" and "Irishman," where we should now write "Gaelic" and "Gael."

With regard to the Macleods, the tradition is general that that family got dominion in Lewis by marriage with the heiress of Mac Nicol; but while willing to believe that Torquil increased his superiority by such marriage, I have shown in the Memoir on Lewis Place-names that Thormod Thorkelson was in Lewis, with wife, men, and goods, in 1231; and that the clan-name, Leod, is in all probability derived from *Liotulfr*, who was a chief in Lewis in the middle of the twelfth century.[4]

[4] "Pro. Soc. Ant. Scot." vol. xi. p. 507.

Of the Morrisons, it is strange that the "Indweller," himself a Morrison, should have ignored what he would have called the "Irish" name of his clan, which is from *Gille-Mhuire, i.e.*, servant of Mary; from *Gille, i.e.*, a servant, &c., and *More, i.e.*, Mary. A Morrison in Gaelic is *Mac Ghillemhuire*, sometimes shortened to Gillmore, Gilmour; or translated Morrison, Maryson; or reduced to Milmore, Miles, Myles. The Morrisons are a numerous clan in Lewis, where, in 1861, they numbered 1402, or one-fifteenth of the whole population; in Harris there were 530, equal to one-seventh of the inhabitants. These numbers indicate a domination in the island of many centuries.

There is no real tradition[5] of their original settlement in Lewis, except

[5] Norman Macleod, "the bard," who believed himself to be acquainted with the builders of the Druidical Circles, and with the origin and history of the Lewis people from the fourth century, told that the Morrisons were originally Macleods [therein agreeing with the ancient genealogy]. The chief of Macleod had a son by a young woman of the name of Mary. The lady of Macleod could not tolerate that one so born should bear the clan-name, so the infant was called "Gille Moiré," the son of Mary; hence the origin of the Morrisons. "I have also sent for another account of the origin of the Morrisons, from a Morrison patriarch, which will doubtless be more honourable than the bard's, the latter being a Macleod" (Letter, Rev. J. M'Rae, Stornoway, 12th Dec. 1860).

that the founder was the inevitable son of the King of Lochlann; but one remarkable genealogy of Macleod makes Gillemuire to have been the father of Leod; and before Raice (Rooke) and Olbair (Ulf ?) the Hewer, we have another Gillemuire. It is added that *Ealga fholt-alainn, i.e.*, Ealga of the Beautiful Hair, daughter of Arailt Mac Semmair, King of Lochlainn, was the mother of Gillemuire."[1]

[1] "Ulst. Jour. Arch." vol. ix. p. 320.

I learn from Mr Skene that the serfs or tenants on lands belonging to a church or monastery dedicated to the Virgin would be called the Gillies of Mary; hence the origin of the name; but in process of time it is evident that such names as Gillemuire were used as proper names, and without any reference to office or employment. Although Petrie says that no Irish churches were dedicated to the Virgin before the twelfth century,[2] there

[2] Round Towers, p. 173. "The dedications to St Mary in Scotland came in long before the 12th century, as early as the sixth."—W. F. Skene.

are notices of Maelmaire, son of Ainbith, at 919 A.D.,[3] and of Maelmuire,

[3] Todd's "Wars of the Gaehhil with the Gaill," p. xci.

son of Eochaidh, abbot-bishop of Armagh, at 1020 A.D.[4] Nor, although

[4] *Ib.* p. clxxxix.

the name is Gaelic, is it to be inferred that the possessor was of pure Gaelic descent, but rather that he was one of the Gall-Gael, or mixed race of Northmen and Gael who peopled the towns and shores of Ireland and the western islands and coasts of Scotland. For Maelmaire, sister of Sitric, King of Dublin, is on record *circa* 1066;[5] and, before the conquest

[5] *Ib.* p. cxlix.

of Ireland, in 1130, Mac Gille Maire, son of Allgoirt of Port Lairge (Waterford), the best foreigner (*Gall*) that was in Eirinn, was slain.[6]

[6] "Chron. Scot." p. 334. And I have seen in a history of Waterford a mandate of protection from Henry II. or III. to Mac Gillvore *and the other Danes* there,—but have lost the reference.

In Ireland there was a Clan Mac Ghillemuire settled in Lecale (*Leth-Cathal*), County Down. On July 7, 1244, Henry III. requests—among others—that Mac Gillemuri himself, and with his forces, will join the Justiciary of Ireland about to depart for Scotland.

The King to [Mac Gillemuri]. Thanks him for the good service he is prepared to render. As Alexander, King of Scotland, has made peace [Mac Gillemuri] may return to his own country, but the king prays he may be ready for service[7] the ensuing summer. For further notices of

[7] Cal. Doc. Ireland, p. 405.

the Clan Mac Ghillemhuire, see Reeves' "Ecc. Antiquities," p. 339.

The chief of the Clan Morrison, whose dwelling was at Habost, Ness, was hereditary judge or brieve[8] (*Breitheamh*) of Lewis, and continued to

[8] The traditionary origin of the title of Brieve of Lewis is absurd. It is that Lewis had been given to Donald Mor Mackay. Donald Mor fell so desperately in love with a daughter of the then Earl of Sutherland that he offered to give Lewis to her if she would be his bride for only one night. She consented, and claimed Lewis, but her pretensions were stoutly resisted by John Morrison. The case went to "head-quarters," when the judge said, "*Ian is tusa Britheamh an fhearann, agus cha ne am boirionach*," *i.e.*, "John, thou art judge of the land, and not this woman." The grain of truth here is, that the mainland estates of the Lewis Macleods were really granted to Mackay in 1508; and for some of the other circumstances compare the traditions in O. S. A. of Edderachyllis.

hold the office till the beginning of the seventeenth century. The only record of his judgeship is that given by Sir R. Gordon, who, under the rubric of "What the office of a Breive is amongst the ilanders,"[9] states

[9] Sir R. Gordon, "Earl of Suth." p. 268, The Supp. to the Conflict of the Clans, has, after "themselfs," "and never doe appeal from his sentence quhen he determineth," &c., p. 12.

that "The Breive is a kind of judge amongst the ilanders, who hath an absolute judicatorie, vnto whose authoritie and censure they willinglie submitt themselves, when he determineth any debatable question betuein partie and partie." In former times there was a brieve in every island, and he had one-eleventh of every subject that was in dispute, but from whom there was an appeal to the chief judge in Islay.[1] Very exaggerated

[1] Coll. De Reb. Alb. p. 297.

notions remain of the extent of the jurisdiction of the brieve of Lewis. One writer asserts that it was a venerable institution that had stood for many ages, and that the jurisdiction extended over the Hebrides from Islay to the Butt of Lewis, and on the opposite coast to the Ord of Caithness; another, that he was invested by His Majesty as judge arbiter from Cape Wrath to the Mull of Kintyre, and was absolute in his jurisdiction.[2]

[2] See also O. S. A. vol. vi. p. 292.

It is probable that the brieve in Lewis represented the loȝ-maðꞃ of Norse domination, and that in the progress of time the office changed from that of law-man or speaker-of-the-law at the þinȝ, or popular assembly, to that of *Dómandi*, or administrator of justice. In the Isle of Man the *Deemster* held an office of great antiquity. He was judge in cases of life and death, as well as in the most trifling contentions. His presence, whether in house or field, on horseback or on foot, constituted a court; his decisions were guided either by what he could remember of like cases, or by his sense of justice, and this *lex non scripta* was called "breast-law." On assuming office he swore that he would administer justice between man and man as evenly as the back-bone of the herring lies between the

two sides of the fish. Wherever the deemster was present, the aggrieved party could lug his opponent before him. The plaintiff placed his foot upon that of the defendant, and held it there till judgment was pronounced. Both in Lewis and in Man the decision seems to have been accepted without reserve.

On the 29th May 1527, King James addressed a letter to "Oure Breff of Inuerness," where "breff" is synonymous with "sheriff;" from whence it may be inferred that the *vice-comes* of Skye, named in the Chronicle of Man, was the brieve of that island. How the office of law-man was abused under Scottish tyranny in Shetland may be seen in Balfour's "Oppressions;" but in Lewis, owing to its remote situation, the brieve appears to have exercised his ancient jurisprudence without interference. It is very doubtful if ever a brieve of Lewis could have spoken a word of English, and as the Scotch Acts of Parliament have not been translated into Gaelic, the decisions of the judge can never have had any relation to them. Before the utter confusion into which the country fell towards the close of the sixteenth century, the brieve of Lewis, like the bard of Clanranald, may have received some education in Gaelic; but in any case we have ample proof that he exercised his office most unsparingly, for there are few islands or districts in which the *Cnoc na Chroiche*, or Gallows Hill,[1] is not a conspicuous feature. With the judge, says Dr Mac Ivor, perished the different records of the Lewis, and of the countries over which he had jurisdiction, except a few memoranda, or rather scraps,[2] retained by some of the judge's descendants who escaped the fury of the Macleods.

The "Indweller" is only partially correct in stating that Kennanus Makurich, *i.e.*, Cain Macvurich (*Cathan Mac Mhurich*), was the first Morrison in Lewis; for the current tradition throughout the island is that the heiress of the Morrisons, having determined she would only marry with a Morrison, Cain, who was a Macdonald from Ardnamurchan, passed himself off for a Morrison, became husband of the lady, and consequently brieve also. The Harris Morrisons claim to be of the original stock. The North Uist historian of the Slate Macdonalds (Hugh Macdonald) states that "Reginald married a brother's son of his grandfather's to an heiress of the name of the Morrisons in the Lewis;" and that Reginald was killed by the Earl of Ross in 1346.[3]

[1] There is a Gallows Hill at Kneep, Uig; at Shawbost, Barvas; another near Stornoway; a *Cnoc na Chroiche* at Scalpay, Harris; and the place where a gallows stood is pointed out at Rodil, Harris. A boat's mast seems to have often been used to hoist up a man instead of a sail, or the mast upon which the victim was suspended was laid across a rift between rocks. Gallows Hill is a common name in the Orkneys and in the Shetland islands.

[2] These scraps were part of a MS. History of the Mackenzies, called by Donald Gregory the Letterfearn MS. Morrison's "Traditions of Lewis" contains what is probably a copy of those scraps.

[3] Coll. De Reb. Alb. p. 292.

No. This was John, Angus Mór's illegitimate son by a daughter of John of Ardnamurchan (HP. I. 16).

The genealogy of the Macdonalds, as given by the Uist historian, when compared with that compiled by Donald Gregory,[4] is found to be confused

[4] "Hist. West. Isles," *passim.*

and inaccurate. Reginald is made to be a son of John, son of Somerled, son of Somerled, the common ancestor of the Macdougals, the Macrories, and the Macdonalds, when, in fact, he was Reginald (Ranald) Mac Rorie, the illegitimate brother of Amie Mac Rorie, who was the first wife of John first Lord of the Isles. For the glorification of his own clan, the Uist historian ignores the existence of the clan Rorie, or wilfully confounds them with the Macdougals, and bastardises them both together.

The John Mac Angus Mor and John Mac Somerled of the Uist historian are the same person; and he is historically known as *Eon Sprangaich*, or John the Bold, son of Angus Môr; he is the founder of the Clan Mac Ian of Ardnamurchan.

It is also stated that John (*Sprangaich*) came to Uist, married a daughter of Macleod of Harris, and had a son named Murdo;[5] and that

[5] De Reb. Alb. p. 291.

from Murdo has descended the ancient branch of the Macdonalds called Shiol Mhurchy. *Mac Mhurich* represents the "Makurich" of Lewis tradition.

It is further stated that Angus Oig of Islay, married a daughter of Guy O'Kaine in Ireland;[6] and this is confirmed by Mac Firbis, who writes

[6] *Ib.* p. 294.

that the mother of John Mac Angus of Islay was *Aine*, daughter of *Cumharghe O' Cathain.*[7] In this way the name of Cain has been introduced—if it was not there before—into the Clan Macdonald, and through them it has been continued as a family name among the Morrisons to the present day.

[7] Hill's "Macdonnells of Antrim," p. 375. 1376, Cumoighe O'Kane, Lord of Oireacht O'Kane (Derry) was taken prisoner by the English at the port of Coleraine, and sent prisoner in fetters to Carrickfergus.—Connellan's "Four Masters."

The conclusion to be drawn is that Kennanus Makurich, *i.e.*, Cain Macvurich, who was adopted into, and from whom descended the leading family of the Morrison's of Ness, was the son of Murdo, son, or rather grandson, of John the Bold, founder of the family of Ardnamurchan; and that the marriage took place not long before 1346.

I am told that the badge of the Morrisons is "drift-wood," of which a great quantity is driven upon the west coast of Lewis. The Lewis word

For "Pat: Mc a Bhriuin" who witnesses the Gaelic Charter of 1408, see Hist. MacDonalds of Isles, 90. But see CPNS, 522.

[illegible] (TGSI, XVI, 58).

For "Donald Brolaiff" (1456) see Mackintosh Muniments, Nos. 3, 5.

For "Hullinhuus Archi-index" of the Isles (1485) see TGSI XXIX. 199.

(x) Long foot note, pp. 292-298.

× See also TGSI, XVI. 40 ff, where it is stated that least of Durness chieftains married a daughter of Donald Ban Matheson of Shiness. [c. 1550]

× Among those granted remission in 1540-1 for the siege of Eilean Donan Castle is "Alexander Makbreif". — Register of Privy Seal II. (Mid Mull Book, 106.)

× Cf. OH, 146. Of the 9 [illegible] [illegible] ... 48, 34[illegible] ... 347 ?.

× Frater Eugenius Makbrehin matriculated at St Andrews University in 1525 (Records of St Andrews University, 220).

for drift-wood is *sgoid*; hence, in derision, a Morrison will be told that he has a "skate" (*sgail*, Gae.) for a baby.[1]

[1] Or, for a wife. Sgoid is undoubtedly a survival of the Norse Skið, a log of timber. "*Sgoid-chladaich*," Gael., a shore [*i.e.*, drift] log.

Besides the district of Ness, the Morrisons were dominant in the district of Diurness, in Lord Reay's country. The tradition of their settlement there is that Ay Mac Hormaid (*Aodh Mac Thormoid*), a Morrison from Lewis, who was a handsome and good-looking fellow, went for a cargo of meal to Thurso, and there married the illegitimate daughter (or the sister) of the Bishop of Caithness, who bestowed upon the young couple the whole of Diurness, with Ashir.[2] Ay Morrison "brought over with him from Lewis a colony of no less than sixty families, mostly of his own name, to whom he gave lands upon his property; hence it is that the name of Morrison is prevalent in these parts, for though the property has fallen into other hands, the stock of the inhabitants remains."[3]

[2] Now foolishly corrupted to "Old Shores." In 1772 it was written Ashar; in 1551, Aslar. In 1263 King Hakon sailed with all his host from the Orkneys to *Asleifar-vik*. Now *Asleifar* becomes *Aslar* by the aspiration of the *f*; and Ashir, the Gaelic form of which would be *Ascar*, by the further aspiration of the *l*. Asleifar-vik is therefore in Loch Inchard (the termination *ard* in which represents the Norse fjorðr), and the *vik* is probably the place now called Badcaul. (I find myself anticipated in this identification, Pope's *Torfæus*, p. 198). The Norse copyists made great mistakes when they had Gaelic names to write. For long it was a puzzle to tell where they got the name of *Satiri* for Kintyre; but it was found once written *Santiri*. This gave the clue, for I do not doubt that hearing the Gaelic *Cean-tir* (Head-land) they wrote originally *Kantiri*, which the copyists have corrupted to Santiri, Satiri. I consider *Hatcrskot* to be a like corruption for Abercros.

[3] O. S. A. vol. vi, Edderachylis; where the tradition of the circumstance which caused the lands to be claimed by the Sutherlands is stated.

In 1518, Mac Ian of Ardnamurchan was killed;[4] the Uist historian says that he fled for the space of a mile, but was overtaken by Mr (*i.e.*, the Master or Heir) Allan Morison, and killed by the Laird of Raisay.[5]

[4] Gregory, "Hist. West. Isles," p. 125.

[5] De Reb. Alb. p. 324.

In 1546–47, March 22, there is a remission to "Rorie M'Cleud of the Lewis," and some of his clan, for treasonable assistance given to "Mathew, formerly Earl of Lennox,"[6] among whom is "William M'huchcon," probably a son of the brieve.

[6] Rec. Privy Seal.—Greg. Colls. MS.

In 1551, July 23, Patrick Davidson is paid £10 by the king's treasurer that he may go to the Lewis to charge "M'Cleude of the Lewis and Hucheon of the Lewis to come to my Lord Govenor [Arran] at the aire at Inverness."[7] This is Hucheon Morrison, brieve or judge of Lewis,

[7] Treasurer's Accts.—Greg. Colls. MS.

There is a summons, dated at Edinburgh, 7th December, 1562, to the MacDonalds of Sleat and their associates for the harrying of the inhabitants of Mull, Tiree, and Coll. In the list of names is that of "Hugo Brief." — *Register of the Privy Seal*, Vol. V. No. 1160.

who was indirectly the cause of the ruin of the *Siol Torquil.*

The Chief of Lewis,[8] Rorie Mac Malcolm Macleod, afterwards known as Old Rorie, had married, when young, Janet Mackenzie,[9] daughter of John Mackenzie of Kintail, and widow of Mackay. She became the paramour of Hucheon Morrison, and on the adultery being known, both she herself and the child she bore—Torquil Connonach (so called from being fostered among his mother's relations in Strath Connan)—were repudiated by Rorie Macleod. He seems to have had sufficient reason, as is shown by the following declaration :—

[8] The following narrative is founded upon Donald Gregory's "History of the Western Highlands and Isles," compared with his "Manuscript Collections," which contain a large amount of interesting matter, and with Sir R. Gordon's "History of the Earls of Sutherland." Besides which Lord Cromartie's "History of the Mackenzies," printed in Fraser's "Earls of Cromartie," has been consulted; as well as two MS. histories of the Mackenzies, &c. &c.

[9] "She was first married to M'Ky, and after his death to this Rory. She had come to a greater age then suited well to his youth, whereupon did shortly follow a dislike, and from dislike to loving of others, whereby in a short time he became wicked, licentious, and putting away his wife, alleging a falsehood, but without process or proof, since they were not grounded on any proof."—Fraser's "Earls of Cromartie," vol. ii. p. 521.

Dr George Mackenzie gives the following account:—Rory Macleod "married Janet Mackenzie, daughter to Kenneth [recté John] the 8th Baron of Kintail, by whom he had Torquil Connonach, to whom he gave the lands of Coigach, but being a man abandoned to all kinds of luxury and vice, and there being no agreement on that account betwixt him and his Lady, the Briff of the Lewis who was the Supreme Judge in all Causes Civil and Ecclesiastical summons him before him to answer for his many notorious adulteries, for he had then in adultery no less than five sons—Tormod, Murdoch, Neil, Donald, and Rory. In revenge of this he accuses the Briff of adultery with his Lady—" &c.—MS. Hist. Mackenzies.

The Letterfearn MS. says nothing about the brieve, but that Mackenzie's daughter was taken away from the Chief of Lewis by his own kinsman, John Mac Gillichally, Laird of Rasay. This statement is adopted by Donald Gregory.

INSTRUMENT[2] UPON THE DECLARATION OF THE BREVE OF LEWIS ANENT THE BIRTH OF TORQUIL, SAID TO BE SON TO M'LEOD OF LEWIS, 22D AUGUST 1566.

[2] From Macleod's Charter Chest.—Greg. Colls. MS.

. . . . The quhilk day Sr Patrik McMaister mairtin Persoun of Barwas deponit upoun his aithe and that he being in Lewiss visiting Hucheoun Breve of Lewess that wes then in the poynt of dethe and in thay dayes wes Confessour to the said Hucheoun attending to the consuetude usit in yai tymes That he sperit and requirit of the said Hucheoun anent yis son Torquill borne be Makkenzes sister as wes allegit to Maccleod of Lewess hir housband Quhat ye said Hucheoun's Jugement wes anent him and to quhome the said Torquill as he belefit pertenit Quha ansuerit to ye said Sr Patrik, yat he cull nocht deny bot he had caiale copulaone wt the said Ne Vc Kenze in hir

husband's tyme in dew tyme and seasoun afoir ye said Torquhillis birthe And y^{t} the s^{d} Huchouns father afoir him tuik w^{t} ye said Torquil to be ye said Huchoun's sone afoir his deathe And in respect that the said Huchoun wes to depairt of this warld in perell of deid he culd not do vtherwayis nor his father afoir him had tane w^{t} the said Torquill That is that the said Hucheoun wes his father naturall And that he culd not refuise him to be sone to him in tymes (comming) And this the said Hucheoun grantit and confessit to ye said Sr Patrik in his Confessioun being in danger of deathe — Upoun ye quhilk confessioun of ye said Sr Patrik and Vidimus of his Testificatioun ane honorabill man Donald Makdonald gorme of Sleat appearand and acclaimand rg^{t} to be air of Lewess Requirit fra me Notar vnderwritten actis and instrumentis befoir yir Witness Ane ry^{t} reverand man Mr Johne Carswell Bischop of ye Iles Hector Makclane Allansoun w^{t} vyeris duierss

Ita est Patriccius Miller

Notarius Publicus &c.

After Rorie Macleod had repudiated his first wife, he married in 1541, Barbara Stewart, daughter of Andrew Lord Avendale, by whom he had a son, Torquil *Oighre* (Torquil the Heir), to whom Queen Mary wrote that he, being of the Stewart blood, should not marry without her consent;[1]

[1] From Inverary, 23d July 1563.

but Torquil Oighre was drowned, somewhere about 1566, when crossing the Minsh. Torquil Connonach then made a claim to succeed, receiving the help of the Clan Kenneth, and no doubt assisted on the island by the Morrisons; he was also supported by two of Rorie Macleod's natural sons, Torquil Uigach (*i.e.*, fostered in Uig) and Murdo, which is easily understood if their mother was a Morrison.

The Castle of Stornoway was taken and the Chief of Lewis made a prisoner for four years. He gives a miserable picture of the treatment he received from his pseudo son. The old chief states that the evil handling he has received from Torquil Connonach and his accomplices these two years bygone is notorious; that his "Lugeing" was invaded by them at night and burnt, himself held in most miserable captivity in mountains and caves far distant from the society of men, and almost perished with cold and hunger.

While still a prisoner, Rorie Macleod was taken to Edinburgh and made, by the friends of Torquil Connonach, to resign his lands to him, Rorie Macleod merely holding them in liferent. But Old Rorie, as soon as he got back to Lewis,[0] repudiated the resignation on the ground of coercion. In 1576, both Old Rorie and Torquil Connonach were summoned before the Regent Morton, when a reconciliation was effected, Old Rorie recognising Torquil Connonach as his heir. In these quarrels three of Old Rorie's natural sons—Neill, Donald, and Rorie Oig—took their father's part, while Tormot Uigach and Murdo sided with the Mackenzies.

Old Rorie, apparently between 1566 and 1570, had taken a third wife, Jennette, the daughter of Maclean, and had by her two sons, Torquil Du and Tormot.

× Clan Iver, 109.

Before long, what Sir Robert Gordon calls "The civill troubles of the Lewis," again commenced. Tormod Uigach, of the Morrison faction, was killed by his brother Donald; for which Donald was seized by Torquil Connonach, with the assistance of Murdo, and carried prisoner to Coygeach, from whence, however, he escaped and got back to Lewis. Old Rorie was incensed against Torquil Connonach for seizing Donald, and caused Donald to apprehend Murdo, who was then imprisoned in Stornoway Castle. Torquil Connonach invaded Lewis, took Stornoway Castle after a short siege, released Murdo, made a prisoner again of his imputed father Old Rorie, killed a number of his men, and carried away all the writs, charters, and infeftments of Lewis; these, on a future occasion, he gave to Mackenzie of Kintail. Torquil Connonach then placed his son John over Lewis, and Old Rorie was, I suppose, a sort of prisoner at large in Stornoway. The date of these transactions is fixed by "Ane Tre maid to Johne M Cloyd oy to Rorie M Cloyd Of ye gift of ye escheit and lyfrent of all guidis &c Quhilkis perteinet to the said Rorie M Cloyd of the Lewis And now pertenis to o^r^ Soureane lord &c Throw being of ye said Rorie odourlie denuncit his Maiestes Rebell and put to ye horne upoun ye xxij day of May, 1583 for non finding of souertie that he sould compeir befoir his Hienes Justice and his Deputes at ane certain day bipast to have under lyne ye lawis for airt and pairt of ye persute of Torquill M Cloyd his sone and apperand aine and divers slauchteris and crymes mentionat and contenit in ye said Tres, &c. &c. Stirling, 20th Sept. 1585."[2]

[2] Gregory Collections, MS.

John Macleod, being in possession, set about banishing his bastard uncles, Rorie Oig and Donald. Rorie Oig having placed an ambuscade, caused John to be deluded out to shoot swans at the Loch of Sandwick, when he was shot himself and killed. Old Rorie was then "agane commander of that iland, which he did possesse dureing the rest of his troublesome dayes."[3]

[3] Sir R. Gordon's "Earls of Sutherland," p. 268.

Malcolm, the father of Old Rorie, died in 1517. Rorie himself appears in record in 1537, and his last appearance is in 1595, in which year he no doubt demised. His least possible age is 78 years, but there is a tradition in Lewis that he was 94 years old when he died.[4]

[4] Dr Macivor, MS.

On the death of Old Rorie, Torquil Du possessed Lewis, excluding Torquil Connonach as a bastard. The mainland estates were held by Torquil Connonach, for which reason they were, in 1596, ravaged by Torquil Du with great barbarity, if Kenneth Mackenzie is to be believed;[1]

[1] Fraser's "Earls of Cromartie," vol. ii. p. 440.

but the young chief, who was followed by 700 or 800 men, appears to have been too powerful to have been conquered by the Mackenzie faction. So a conspiracy was entered into by Kenneth Mackenzie, Torquil Connonach, John Morrison the brieve of Lewis, and Murdo, when it was considered necessary that Torquil Du "should be maid out of the way: bot," says Sir R. Gordon, "ther laiked ane to execute the interpryse."[2] At

[2] The fragment of Sir R. Gordon's Hist. of the Earl. of Sutherland in the *Miscellanea Scotica* is printed from an earlier and better MS. than that of the Edinburgh edition of 1813. In the "Conflict," Donald Mac Neill "went into Holland, quher he remains" (p. 27); in the Edinburgh edition it is "wher he died" (p. 276). The paragraph relating to the conspiracy of Mackenzie in the "Conflict," is—"Kenneth M'Kenzie of Kintail, (afterwards Lord of Kintail,) Torq. Conn., Murdo M'Leod baise brother of Torq. Conn., and the Briewe of the Lewes, (the son of that Briewe [Hucheon Morrison] who was said to be the father of Torq. Conn.,) haid a secret meiting together, to consult of ther affaires; the Lord Kintail his proposition was, that to advance Torq. Conn. to the possession of the Lewes, it was requisit that his brother Torq. Dow should be maid out of the way, which motion was presently embraced by the rest, but ther laikit on to execut the enterpryce" (p. 15).

length the brieve, by the promise of a great reward, was induced to undertake the matter. John Morrison having soon afterwards captured a Dutch ship partly laden with wine, he took his prize to Stornoway, and invited Torquil Du to come on board to partake of a banquet. But instead of wine they bring them cords, and Torquil Du and his company were carried across to Ullapool, to Torquil Connonach, where Kenneth Mackenzie caused them all to be beheaded, in July 1597. At the instant of execution there was an earthquake, which much astonished the malefactors, though naturally hardened by cruelty and mischief.[3]

[3] Here the text in the "Conflict" is better than that of the Edinburgh edition, for we get the information in the former that Torquil Du had but seven men in company (p. 15).

The Lewis estates had been made over to Kenneth Mackenzie, as far as writings could do it, by Torquil Connonach; the Government made Lewis over to adventurers; but the command of the island was possessed by the bastard uncle, Neil Macleod.

The Mackenzie faction, having failed to gain Lewis, left the Morrisons exposed to the vengeance of the Macleods for their treachery to Torquil Du; but the foregoing narrative supplies a reason for their conduct. The oligarchic Sir R. Gordon, cannot imagine that the ties of blood should be superior to fealty to a chief. About this time the Morrisons fortified themselves in Dun Eystein, at Ness.

Dun Eystein is a natural stronghold at the north end, or Ness, of Lewis, in the townland of *Cnoc Aird*, to which the Morrisons were wont to retire when hard pressed or in times of war. It is a flat, cliffy island, of a somewhat oval shape, about 75 yards long and 50 yards broad, and is separated from the mainland by a narrow, perpendicular ravine, through which the sea flows at high water. The ravine is between 30 and 40 feet broad, and the same in height. The remains of a strong wall follows the edge of the cliff on the landward side of the island, and through the wall there is said to have been squints or loopholes for observation and defence.

x <u>MacLeods</u>, 404, 406.

Towards the north-east corner of the island is a dûn or castle, sometimes called *Tigh nah Arm*; or the House of Arms, now but 4½ feet high. The outside of the dûn is an oblong square, 23 by 18 feet; and this basement is nearly solid, for the central area, which is of an oval shape, is only 6½ by 4½ feet, and there is no appearance of any doorway. The entrance or doorway was no doubt at the height of the first floor, similar to a dûn in Toransay. The walls are of dry-stone masonry, but that is no proof of age in this part of the country. When exploring the ruins, the Rev. M. Macphail, who made the above measurements, found a small piece of flint, fragments of charcoal, and a strip of leather such as was used for making brogues.

There are the remains of huts upon the island; and on the south sides is a flat ledge, called *Pulla*[1] *na Biorlinn*, or the Ledge of the Galley or Birlin, whereon tradition tells that the Morrisons used to haul up their boat.

[1] This interesting word is a survival from the Norse, and means in Lewis "a grassy ledge in a cliff." Cf. Cleasby's "Icel. Dic.," *sub voce* "*Pallr.*"

There is no tradition of the Eysteinn who gave his name to the dûn; it is a common Norse name.

Many sanguinary battles, still recounted by tradition, were fought between the Macleods and Macaulays on one side, and the Morrisons on the other. At last the Morrisons were forced to leave Lewis, and take refuge with that branch of their clan which was settled in Duirness and Edderachyllis, in Sutherland, where still, in 1793, the natives were all, except a few, of the three names of Mac Leay, Morrison, or Macleod.

At that time there lived on *Eilean Shanvlaidh* (pronounced Elen Handa), *i.e.*, Sandey or Sand Island, one of the family of Assynt Macleods, named Little John Mac Donald Vic Hucheon, a man of low stature, but of matchless strength and skill in arms. He and the brieve, John Morrison, met accidentally in a house in Inverkirkaig in Assynt. Being in one room and of contrary factions, presently they fell to fighting, when, although the brieve had six men, and John of Sandey but four, the brieve

X. Led by Tormod Uigeach MacLeod.

⊗ Quoted *in extenso*, HP II. 273.

and five of the Morrisons were killed without any loss on the side of the Macleods. Sir R. Gordon suggests that God deprived the brieve and his company of the courage or ability to resist; but it must not be forgotten that this same John of Sandey had been previously defeated at Carloway, in Lewis, by the Morrison faction.[1]

[1] Sir R. Gordon's "Hist. of Earl. Suth.," pp. 264, 272; O. S. A., vol. vi. pp. 292, 293.

Among the numerous islands on the coast of Edderachyllis is one called *Eilean a Bhritheimh*, or Judge's Island; for after John Morrison had been slain his friends in Lewis came in a galley to bring home his corpse; but contrary winds arising, they were driven to this island, where they found it convenient to disembowel the body and bury the intestines, and on the wind changing they arrived in safety at Ness.[2]

[2] O. S. A., vol. vi. p. 293.

Malcolm Mòr Mac Ian, who now succeeded to the chieftainship of the Morrisons, sought for John of Sandey, in order to revenge the death of his father, when both parties met by chance in Coygeach. They fought; but John of Sandey, besides killing most of the opposite party, took Malcolm Mòr himself prisoner, and carried him to Tormod Macleod in Lewis, who caused him to be beheaded. This was between 1601 and 1605.

In October 1599 the Fife adventurers, with 500 or 600 soldiers, artificers, &c., sailed for Lewis, when Murdo Macleod captured the Laird of Balcolmy near the Orkneys, where soon afterwards the unfortunate gentleman died. Neil and Murdo opposed the adventurers in Lewis; but Murdo had all along supported the Morrison faction, while Neil represented the Macleods. The brothers soon quarrelled, and Neil took Murdo prisoner. The adventurers offered to Neil, if he would deliver Murdo to them, that they would procure Neil's pardon, and give him a portion of the island. Neil accepted these terms, went with the adventurers to Edinburgh, taking with him the heads of ten or twelve Morrisons,[3] and had his pardon. Murdo, against whom the adventurers must have been much exasperated for causing the death of Balcolmy, was also carried south and hanged at St Andrews; "who, at his death, reveiled something of the Lord of Kintayle his proceedings. Then the king was advertised by the adventurers, that the Lord of Kintayle was a crosser and hinderer of their interpryse; wherevpon he was brought in question, and was committed to warde in the castell of Edinburgh, from whence he escaped without his tryall, by means and credet of the Lord Chancelar of Scotland."

In 1601 the adventurers and Neil M'Leod returned to Lewis, but they soon became enemies; an attempt being made to entrap Neil, he, being aware of their purpose, surprised the party sent against him, and killed sixty of their number. Mackenzie then let loose Tormod Macleod (the youngest son of Old Rorie), whom he had abducted from school in Glasgow and held prisoner and hostage against the Siol Torquil and his mother's relations the Macleans. Mackenzie secretly promised the young man great assistance if he would attack the settlers in concert with his uncle.

As soon as Tormod got to Lewis he was at once acknowledged by the islanders as their chief; he speedily attacked the camp of the adventurers, and forced them to capitulate. They agreed to obtain a remission from the king for all past offences of the Macleods; that they would not return to Lewis, but give up their title to the island to Tormod; and that they would surrender Sir James Spence and his son-in-law, Thomas Monypenny of Kinkell, as hostages, till these conditions were fulfilled.

The remission seems to have been procured; but the adventurers only waited till their hostages were out of danger before they prepared for the reconquest of the island.

In 1605 the adventurers returned, with extreme legal powers and a great force, to Lewis. The adventurers offered Tormod to procure his pardon from the king, and not to oppose any grant he could obtain to afford him the means of subsistence. Tormod was sent to London; but when it was understood that his—or his nephew's—claim to Lewis was likely to be regarded with favour, the adventurers, by means of their friends at court, prevailed so far that Tormod was sent down to Edinburgh, where this victim of untoward circumstances was detained a prisoner for ten years.

Tormod Macleod had submitted to the terms of the adventurers against the advice of his uncle Neil; and Neil still opposed them, being assisted by Macneil of Barra, the captain of Clanranald and Macleod of Harris—who were all in fear that their estates would be likewise confiscated—and being secretly supported by Mackenzie, the adventurers became weary of

[3] "There wase ane vther conwention appointed to hold heir at Edinburgh, vpone the first of Aprylle 1599; wherin ther was a contract part betwixt the Kings Majestie and gentlemen venturers towards the Lewes, vpone certaine conditions, speciallie, that sufficient securitie being maid to them therof, they sould pay to his Majestie sewin scoire chalders of beare yairlie. And vndertaking the journey toward the Lewes in the end of October the same yeare, accompanied with v or vi [c] men vnder vadges, besyde gentlemen woluntars, throw the coldness of the ile, the lake of ludgeinge, and vther enterteinment, a number of them died of fluxes. And the laird of Balcombie and his cumpanie, passinge in ane boate out of the Lewes toward Orkenay, were intercepted be the way be sume hilandmen supposed to be Mackenzies men, be whome sume of Balcombies men was slaine, and himself taken and detained captive, and so hardlie vsed, that be deadlie diseases contractit he deceasit in Orknay after he wes sett at libertie. Be the meanes of ane speciall hielandman off that ile there were ten or twelfe apprehendit of the speciall withstanders of that interpryse, and beheidit, and ther heids sent heir in a pok to Edinburgh, which were sett vpone the ports thereof."—Moysie's "Memoirs," p. 165 (Bann. Club).

† In 1599 (*ante*). But Allan Morison on record in 1600.

[x] Donald Mac Iain Duibh the Brieve 1613 + 1616 (*Mackenzies*, 226, 228, 234). ∞ Died 1628. † *Mackenzies*, 228.
[RPC X. 4, 610.]

Donald McIndowie Breiff. – RPC X. 692 (1613); 697 (1614). [r (692)]

their undertaking, forsook the island, and returned home.

Mackenzie now, acting upon a resignation formerly made to him by Torquil Connonach, got a charter of Lewis to himself passed under the great seal by means of his son's father-in-law, the Lord Chancellor. But the adventurers complained to the king, who forced Mackenzie to resign the gift; and the island being once more at the disposal of his Majesty, he granted it anew to three persons only. In 1609 these adventurers again landed in Lewis, and Mackenzie proposed to supply them with provisions by a ship from Ross-shire; but at the same time he gave secret information and instructions to Neil Macleod, who captured the ship. The adventurers, being short of provisions, dismissed their forces and returned southwards, but left a garrison in their fort—which I am told was at the point of Holm, where certainly the remains of ramparts and trenches still exist. Neil Macleod soon captured and burned the fort, but sent the garrison out of the island unhurt. This was the last attempt of the Lowlanders to colonise the Lewis, and, being disgusted with their failure, they were easily persuaded to sell their rights to Mackenzie, who then, July 20, 1610, acquired a legal title to Lewis. The Mackenzies then sent a large force into the island, to which the islanders made no resistance, except Neil Macleod and his nephews, and about thirty others, who fortified a rocky island in the mouth of Loch Roag, and there defied the powers of the Mackenzie for nearly three years. But, in 1612, "the Clan Cheinzie gathered their wyffs and children of those that were in Berrisay,[1] and such as, by way of affinitie or consanguinity, within the island, did apperteyn to Neill and his followers, and placed them all vpon a rock within the sea, wher they might be heard and sein from the rock of Berrisay. They vowed and protested that they wold suffer the sea to overwhelme them the nixt flood if Neill did not presentlie surrender the fort; which pitifull spectacle did so move Neill Macloyd and his company to compassion, that immediatlie they yielded the rock, and left the Lewes; whereupon the women and children were rescued and randered."[2]

Neil took refuge in Harris, but shortly presented himself before Sir Rorie Macleod of Harris, and requested to be taken to the court of the king in England. To this Sir Rorie consented, and they had arrived as far as Glasgow on their journey, when Sir Rorie was met by a mandate from the Privy Council to deliver up Neil to them; and the last of the Siol Torquil who led the clan in arms was hanged in Edinburgh, in April 1613.[3] And so ended the "Troubles in the Lewis."

As noted above, those of the Brieve's descendants[4] who had escaped the fury of the Macleods took refuge with the portion of their clan that was settled in Lord Reay's country. When the Mackenzies had gained possession of Lewis, the relatives of the Brieve returned and established themselves again at Ness. According to tradition, John the Brieve, who was killed at Inverkarkaig, had four sons,—Allan, Donald, Kenneth, and Angus. A fifth was Malcolm Mor, who was beheaded at Stornoway. Allan and two others are said to have been killed in a sea-fight by Neil Macleod, and their heads were probably taken by Neil Macleod to Edinburgh, where he himself was afterwards hanged. Of Donald we appear to have authentic record; for in a commission of Fire and Sword, dated 24th June 1630, granted to "Rorie M'Kenzie of Cogach, Tutor of Kintaill," and others, against the remaining members of the Siol Torquil. "Donald M'Indowie [Donald Macillevore] Brieff" is included, and this is the last notice I have found of the *Brieve* of Lewis.

× See Mackenzies, ut supra.

Donald, along with some Macleods, is described as having been concerned in the first rebellion against the Gentlemen Adventurers; but it is difficult to understand why a Morrison, whose clan had suffered so severely for having favoured the Mackenzies, was included in the commission of extermination. It is repeatedly affirmed that the Morrisons assisted the

[1] Berisay (Berrisay, Berinsay (misprint for Berirsay), Birsay), in Gaelic orthography *Bereasaidh*, for *Byrgis-ey*, Norse, = Enclosed or Fortified-island; from *Byrgi*, Norse, = an enclosure, fence; and *Ey*, Norse, = an island. The name is identical with Birsa, in the Orkneys. *Byrgi*, an entrenchment, is repeated in "The Berry," Hoy, Orkney; at *An Berigh*, Shabost, Lewis; and a *Loch na Beridh*, Benbecula.

A gulf, or estuary, full of islands, on the west side of Lewis, has (like Loch Tarbert, Harris) lost its distinctive Norse name, and has acquired that of Loch Roag, though that name really belongs to a narrow inlet or voe (*voagr*), now called Little Loch Roag, in the entrance to which there is a dangerous *strom* or rapid, which is the *Rok* (Norse, for a foaming, splashing sea). There is another *Rok* (Roag) in Skye.

The greater part of Loch Roag is nearly filled by the large island of Bernera (*Bjarnar-ey*); and off the north end of Bernera, in the open sea, are a number of small islands, and among them is Berisay. It was at sunset, on an autumn evening, that I pulled past this island-fortress, and I had every wish to examine the scene of nearly the last act in the bloody drama of the "Conquest of the Lewis;" but the sea was up, it was already nearly dark, and my vessel was several miles away, so after a good look at its craggy sides, I steered for Loch Carloway. It seemed a dreadful place to live on, for in winter there must be weeks and even months in which, by reason of the raging sea, no boat could land upon it; yet it was here a brave, treacherous, and bad man held out against the superior fraud and violence of the Clan Kenneth.

Berisay is a craggy islet, one-tenth of a mile long and half as broad, surrounded by mural cliffs 100 feet high, with an *acarsaid* or landing-place on the south-east side, and the ruins of huts upon the *terre plein;* the highest part of the rock is 175 feet above the sea. Berisay is exposed to the whole force of the Atlantic Ocean, but is beau ideal of a pirate's nest, commanding a view of half the horizon, impregnable, and near a frequented harbour.

[2] Sir R. Gordon's "Earl of Sutherland," p. 275.

[3] The Macleods of Rasay thereafter inherited the chieftainship of the Siol Torquil; and I was told by the late Rev. Rory Macleod of Snizort that the head of that family was then a billiard-marker in London.

[4] "The banker in Stornoway [the late Mr Roderick Morrison], is the 7th or 8th in descent from the last of them;" *i.e.*, the Brieves of Lewis.—*Letters*, Rev. John M'Rae, Stornoway, 12th Dec. 1860.

x "Thirty years bygone" before 1726*, i.e. 1696 (F.E.P.).

⊗ There were two leading Papists in Lewis at the time: John Mackenzie of Assynt, and George Mackenzie of Kildun. Capt. Thomas has confused the two.

Mackenzies to reduce Lewis, but a slight explanation is offered by one of the bards,[1] who states that the "Soldier of Kintail promised part of Kintail to Donald, but never gave it."

Towards the end of the seventeenth century the whole of Lewis formed but two parishes—Barvas and Ey (Stornoway). The minister of Barvas was the Rev. Donald Morrison, who must have been born about 1620; he was a grandson of the judge, was bred an Episcopalian minister, but conformed to Presbyterianism. He was personally known to Martin, and supplied that invaluable writer with information about North Rona. Mr Donald helped to suppress the sacrifice to *Shony*[2] about 1670, and died before 1700. in his 86th year. He was succeeded in Barvas by his son, the Rev. Allan Morrison.[3]

When Mr Donald was minister of Barvas, his brother, Rev. Kenneth Morrison, was minister of Stornoway; he joined with his brother in suppressing the sacrifice to *Shony*, and informed Martin of a singular method which he saw practised in his own church for exorcising the second-sight from a "Maid."[4] He also conformed to the Presbyterian Church. Mr Kenneth was a highly gifted man, and well suited to repress the turmoils in Lewis which then existed between the Papists and Protestants; for he used to walk from his manse at Tong to the church at Stornoway with his sword at his side, and when preaching he had two men standing with drawn swords at the door of the church.

The Papists received great encouragement from John Mackenzie of Assynt (who was a Papist), Laird of Kildun, and uncle of William, Earl of Seaforth. They kept Mr Kenneth so much on the alert that he never went to bed without having his sword lying by him. On one occasion the Laird of Kildun was so exasperated against the minister that he sent six stout men to bring Mr Kenneth by force to Aignish, where he then resided. The men arrived at the manse just as Mr Kenneth had gone to bed; his wife suspected some evil design, and informed her husband. He merely told her to send them up stairs if they had any business with him. They were brought to his room and on his asking them what they wanted they told him that the Laird had bid them take him to Aignish.[5] He replied, "Oh, very well; let us first drink the Laird's health, and then I will go with you." To this there was no objection. Now Mr Kenneth had a very large "dram-horn,"[6] which was only used on particular occasions; and it was now produced. The men drank the Laird's health, and then that of his lady. His reverence then asked them to drink his own health. By this time the men were so exhiliarated that they would drink anybody's health. But John Barleycorn was master of them, and they were soon unable to move hand or foot. Mr Kenneth then made his own men bind them with ropes of straw, carry them to the boat, ferry them to Aignish, and lay them in the passage leading to the Laird's room. The Laird was restless from anxiety, and rose early to learn what success had attended his adventure, and, on going out, stumbled over one of his drunken men. They could give no account of how they came there, nor why they were bound with straw in so ridiculous a manner. The Laird said this was black Kenneth's doing, and that he had practised some trick to bring them to that condition; but that they should be thankful to Mr Kenneth for not having left them on the shore within reach of the flood.

The clemency of Mr Kenneth softened in some degree the anger of the Laird, for shortly afterwards he wrote to Mr Kenneth to come to Aignish to have a discussion on the merits of their respective creeds. Mr Kenneth was kindly received, and after dinner the discussion took place. Mr Kenneth seems to have advanced his arguments with moderation, and illustrated them with amusing stories, by which the Laird was induced to assert that he would more minutely examine into the doctrines of his Church. From that time the Laird moderated his zeal for the Papists, and

[1] Angus Gunn, North Dell, Ness.

[2] This remarkable superstition—of making an offering at Hallowmas to a supposed sea-god, that he might send a plentiful supply of sea-weed on shore—and which was supposed to have been abandoned about 1760, must have been the survival of the *haust-blót*, or autumnal sacrificial feast of the pagan Scandinavians; for *Sjóni* is a name derived from *són*, = an atonement, sacrifice (of the heathen age) (Cleasby's Iced. Dic. pp. 535, 586). *Onundr Sjóni* is named in the *Land bóta*, pp. 73, 89. But although the sacrifice to *Shony* may have been repressed the superstition only took another form; for up to quite recent times there existed an almost extinct custom of proceeding in spring to the end of a long reef, and there mocking "*Briannil*," "*Brianvilt*," to send a strong north wind and drive plenty of sea-ware on shore to manure the land.

There seemed little prospect of making anything out of "*Brianuil, Brianuilt*," until the Rev. M. Macphail told me that "*Brianuilt*" was the name of a saint, and that his day was about the 26th or 27th May. Now, St Brenden is written in Irish, *Brenainn*, and Martin calls St Brendan's Chapel in St Kilda *St Brianan;* this day is on the 16th May; and if this is taken as Old Style his festival would be on 28th May, New Style.

With regard to the terminations *uil, uilt*, I hazard the conjecture that they represent the Gaelic *Scòladair* = sailor, voyager; for when written phonetically it is *Shulta*, and when compounded *ulta;* so that *Brianuilt* I take to be a condensed form of *Breanaian-sheoladair, i.e.*, Brendan the Voyager.

There is a legend among the Lewis folk which implies that the "Temple" on Sulasgeir was erected by or dedicated to St Brendan; but the inference is countervailed by the fact that the island is known as "Bara," which surely means the Island of St Barr.

3 Rev. Mr Gunn, formerly of ~~Loch~~; MS. But the O. S. A. has "Murdoch" Morrison.

[4] Martin's "Western Isles," p. 314.

[5] Aignish, for *Eggja-nes*, Norre Egg-ness, so called from the rounded pebbles found on its shores. Aignish forms the south-east point of Loch Stornoway.

[6] "Dram-horn," in Gaelic *Adharc-dhrama*. The one I have is a section of a cow's horn, 3½ inches high, and 2¼ inches across the mouth; it holds 3¼ fluid ounces or about one-third of a tumbler. How large one might be that was only used on particular occasions it would be rash to guess.

⊗ Another daughter, Janet, was married to John Campbell (*Iain liath*) of Strond, Harris. — *Macleans of Boreray*, 117. (This statement is unreliable, and, as Iain liath is on record in 1614, it cannot be true.) But note that in Morison MSS. there is a reference to Angus Campbell of Ensay as the son of "John Gray Campbell". So there may have been two ~~[illegible]~~ Campbells, each known as *Iain liath*. Neither of them, however, can have been married to a daughter of Rev. Kenneth Morison. But the daughter of the Rev. Donald Morison, minister of Stornoway, was Mrs Campbell, and she may have been the wife of the above John Campbell of Ensay (Unlikely: she appears to have been destitute) — *Lewis Presbytery Records*.) She was, in fact married to Kenneth Campbell, Surveyor of the Customs, Stornoway (*The Blind Harper*, 189).

lived on good terms with Mr Kenneth.

The Rev. Kenneth Morrison was a good poet, as some of his productions in the Gaelic language sufficiently attest. The Rev. Aulay Macaulay, minister of Harris, married a daughter of the Rev. Kenneth Morrison.

Mr Kenneth was succeeded as minister of Stornoway by his second cousin, the Rev. Donald Morrison, whose pedigree is thus given: Donald MacRorie Vic Angus Vic Allan *Mhic an Breitheimh; i.e.* son of the brieve (John Morrison). Mr Donald must have lived till 1747, when his successor the Rev. John Clark, was admitted.[1]

It is told that Mr Donald studied at St Andrews, where having won the good opinion of the professors they recommended him to the notice of William, Earl Seaforth, who presented him to the church of Stornoway. Mr Donald was zealous in his calling; in no long time he married a lady of great personal attractions; Seaforth, the young Laird of Kildun, and many others were at the wedding. That night nothing but politics were discussed, and they all got early to bed. Seaforth invited Mr Donald, his bride, and all the party to come next day to Seaforth Lodge, where there was a splendid and cheerful feast. The Rev. Kenneth Macaulay, minister of Harris, but a Lewis man, was present.

Seaforth himself was a Protestant, but the Lard of Kildun and some others were rank Papists, and they determined to browbeat the two ministers. A smart discussion ensued; but it is a Protestant who reports the arguments, so of course the Protestants had the best of it.

Not long afterwards Mrs Morrison became unruly in her family, when it was found out that the cause of Mrs Morrison's change from better to worse was the effect of spirits. Mr Donald was unable to reform his wife, so that her habitual intemperance became known far and wide, and the clergy threatened to suspend him for not separating from such a woman. He received a letter from the Synod to appear before it. By the advice of Seaforth he wrote to his relation, the Rev. Angus Morrison (of Contin), who was then living at *Doire-na-muic*, by Little Loch Broom. Mr Angus gave Mr Donald a sealed letter, dated 1741, to the moderator of the Synod; but in spite of argument the Synod summoned Mr Donald before the General Assembly. The two friends went to Edinburgh, and there engaged the services of John Macleod of Muiravonside, advocate. After hearing arguments from both sides, the Assembly decided against the Synod.

Some months after Mr Donald had returned to Stornoway, on a Sunday after coming from church, he was reading the Bible while Mrs Morrison was brawling and annoying all the family. But the minister was deaf to her noise, and would take no notice of her; this so enraged Mrs Morrison that she snatched the Bible off the table and threw it in the fire. His reverence preserved his composure, and, drawing his chair close to the fire and warming his hands, he said, "Well, mistress; this is the best fire I ever warmed myself at." Mrs Morrison gazed at her husband and at the Bible in the flames; without saying anything she withdrew to another room, and from that hour, to the joy of all around her, she became sober and penitent, and strove daily to add to the comfort of her husband and family.[2]

In 1653, Murdo Morrison, son of Allan, son of the brieve (John) was tacksman of Gress. He had three sons—John, subsequently known as the tacksman of Bragar, Allan, and Murdo.

x cf Bernera

On the 10th August 1653, Colonel Cobbett of the Roundhead army took possession of the peninsula on which the town of Stornoway now stands, and having had the arms of the place delivered up to him, he fortified the point and left Major Crispe as governor of Lewis, with six companies of soldiers, two great guns, and four sling pieces. On 31st January 1654, a strange report reached Edinburgh, that Seaforth had with 1400 men stormed the fort of Stornoway and taken it. But on 14th February 1654, more certain information arrived there, and "the business of Lewis was thus—Norman [rectè John] Macloud [of Rasay, and nephew of Seaforth] with four or five hundred men, landed in the Lewis island [at Loch Shell], and after three or four days staying at some inaccessible places in the isle, fell upon our soldiers who lay at Stornoway out of the fort, and killed twelve of them; but a party out of the fort beat them thence, relieved the remainder of the men, removed the goods into the fort and burnt the houses." On 21st March news arrived at Dalkeith, that "the garrison of Lewis had made slaughter of the country people that joyned with Seaforth, and they have also slaughtered some of the garrison; the old natives [Macleods] joyned with our men against the rest of the country, so that these divisions cause great devastation in those parts."[3]

This account is corroborated by the "Indweller,"[4] but the patriotic antiquists now tell a very different story which need not be repeated here; except that John, the future tacksman of Bragar, being on good terms with the officers of the garrison, spent the night previous to the attack in drinking with them, and after observing where the sentinels were posted and the weakest part of the defence, returned to Gress. His brother Allan had been employed in collecting the Lewis men. The attack was made at night in two columns; Seaforth marching by the lands of Torry, and Rasay by Bayhead.[5] The result is stated above.

John Morrison of Bragar, who is said to have had "Ladies modesty, Bishops gravity, Lawyers eloquence, and Captains conduct,"—was personally known to Martin, and described by him of "a person of unquestionable sincerity and reputation;" and is still remembered for his poetry, shrewdness, and wit. He is named by Martin at pp. 28, 315, and 316 of the "Western Isles."

[1] O. S. A., vol. xix. p. 250; Culloden Papers, p. 293.
[2] Morrison's "Traditions of Lewis."
[3] Spot. Mis., vol. ii. pp. 124, 126, 169, 196.
[4] Ib., p. 342.
[5] Dr Macivor, M.S.

A great part of the lands of Bragar was, as was universal at that time, sublet to tenants. It happened that Seaforth sent for Morrison to come to Stornoway; it was spring time, and Morrison was in doubt as to whom he should leave in charge of the farm during his absence. In order to fix upon the most trustworthy, he took the following plan:—He closed up all the windows and openings that admitted light, and placed a big stone in the passage that led to his room. He then sent to tell all his tenants that he had something to say to them. The tenants arrived, each one stumbling over the stone, till at last an old man, after sprawling across the passage, remarked that that was no place for such a stone, and rolled it out of the way. John Morrison then said to his tenants, "You may now go away all of you; but while I am absent see you obey the instructions of this old man, who I leave as my substitute, and who appears to be the most careful and willing of you all."

One day John Morrison had the people of Balaloch, in Bragar, working on his farm. They had their breakfast at his house, but lingered too long over it. When they resumed their work, he addressed them thus:—

Fasan muintir Balaloch,
An deigh mo chuid arain is brochain ith 'us òl.
Na h-uile feard'begeart éiridh,
'S cha togadh e féin thon.

As much as to say that it was the way of the people of Balaloch, after eating his bread and drinking his *brochan*,[1] for each to say it is time for us to go to work, but that no one got up from his seat.

On one occasion John Morrison considered himself overcharged by the factor, and refused to pay his demand. The factor complained to Seaforth, who sent for Morrison to come to Stornoway. Morrison set out at once, putting the rent into one purse and what he considered to be the overcharge in another. When he arrived at Seaforth Lodge a large dog barked furiously at him, on which Morrison struck it a violent blow on the nose with his stick. The dog yelled dismally, and one of Seaforth's servants, on coming to see what was the matter, commenced to abuse Mr Morrison, who punished his insolence by striking him on the jaw. The uproar now was greater than ever, and Seaforth made his appearance. John Morrison explained the origin of the row, and added:—

Gille tighearna ' us cù mòr.
Dithis nach còir leigidh leò;
Buail am balach air a' charbaid.
'S buail am balgair air an t-sròin.

Translation.

The boy (menial) and bull-dog (watch-dog) of a laird
Are two that should not be let alone;
Strike the boy on the jaw,
And strike the dog on the nose.

[illegible] No. 245

[illegible], Mr 89; CC, 132

Seaforth was amused at Morrison's impromptu verse, and welcomed him cordially. Morrison told him why he had not paid the rent, and presented the bags containing the real rent and what he had been overcharged. On inquiry, it was found that the factor exacted more rent than was just, and he was dismissed, while John Morrison had the honour of paying his rent in future into Seaforth's own hands.

John Morrison sent two of his servants to pull heather for making ropes; one pulled indiscriminately whatever came in his way, whether fit or unfit; the other left a great deal of soil sticking to the roots. When John Morrison saw what they had done, he said:—

Chuir me breinean'us fuididh
'Bhuain fraoich an cuideachda chéile ;
Thug breinean dhachaidh an cudhrom,
'S thug fuididh dhachidh na geugan.

Translation.

I sent Nasty and Turbulent
To pull heather in company together;
Nasty brought home dandriff,
And Turbulent brought home [only] bare sticks.

John Morrison had a red-haired wife, who was sometimes in a bad temper, and on whom he occasionally practised his sarcastic humour, as follows:—

Diubhaidh connaidh fearna fhliuch;
Diubhaidh side flion chur ;
'S gus an téid an saoghal as
'Se diubhaidh an t-saoghail droch bhean.

Translation.

The worst of fuel is wet alder;
The worst of weather is soft sleat;
And until the world is at an end
The worst thing in it is a bad wife.

Again:—

Fadadh teine ann an loch;
'Tiormachadh cloich ann an cuan;
Comhairle ga toirt air mnaoi bhuirb
Mar bhill' uird air iarrunn fuar.

[1] *Brochan*, Gael., thin gruel.

× [illegible] of Dalbeg ([illegible])

Chuireadh Dùghall bho 'n a' phraca
Mar nach {dèanadh e dad a / glacadh e bho neach i} riamh,
'S mar e Mac Amhlaidh as ceart(a)
Clù gach neach sin le ghnìomh. (<u>MacNeil</u> <u>MSS.</u>)

"Domhnall a' Chnaim was an old bachelor, who had nothing to do but to go rock and loch fishing, and when lucky to get some fish and gorge himself, he would go and lie on the hillside. In this position he was when John Morrison composed the above lines for him." – <u>MS.</u> of <u>Rev.</u> <u>Angus</u> <u>Macleod</u>, <u>Knock</u>.

Translation.

Making a fire in a lake;
Drying a stone in the ocean;
Giving advice to a headstrong wife
Is like the stroke of a hammer on cold iron.

It appears to have been the custom in Lewis for the ground-officer (under-bailliff—*maor*, in Gaelic) to have claimed half the smith's dues. Donald MacRoric was then ground-officer, and his demand was resisted by Murdo Morrison. His father pleaded his cause very pithily, as follows:—

Aon do charaibh an t-saoghail
Saoilidh mi féin gu 'm beil e tuadhal;
Gobha ga losgadh an ceardach
'S leth na cain aig Domhuil Mac Ruairdh:

meaning that he thought the world must be turning round the wrong way; for Donald Mac Rorie to take half the *cain* (tax dues) while the smith was being scorched in his smithy.

John Morrison had to pay some tax in Stornoway, and sent it by Donald Chuain, a poor man who sometimes worked on his farm. When Donald came back, John Morrison went to Donald's house, where he found him leaning on his elbow in bed. When John Morrison was leaving, he said:—

'S buidhe dhuit fein Dhomhuill Chuain
'S tu ad laidhe air do chluain thaobh;
Cha thog pracadair do gheall,
'S cha mho tha thu an taing na maoir.
Dh' fhalbh thu s' cha mhist leam
'S dh' fhag thu mo lionn agam fein
'S leis a bhith bha nam fheòil
Dheaninn òl ged dheidheadh tu eig.

Translation.

Happy art thou, oh! Donald of the Main,
Reclining easy on your side;
A tax-gatherer will not sue thee for taxes,
Nor to a *maor* (ground-officer) you need not crouch.
You have left, and I do not care.
And you have left—to me—all my ale;
And by the desire that is in my flesh
I would drink though you should die.

Meaning that he does not care what becomes of Donald, as he has a good stock of ale; and that he is so thirsty that he would not go without a drink to save Donald's life.'

Donald of the Ocean is immortalized by Martin; for he tells us Donald lived in a village near Bragar, and that he cut his toe at the change of the moon (perhaps on this very journey), "and it bleeds a fresh drop at the change of the moon ever since."—"West. Isles," p. 13.

× 1670. See TGSI, xxiv. 376; *Highland Monthly*, I. 485. According to the latter source the date was July, 1672; and this is confirmed by the place and date of a bond of friendship between Kenneth, Earl of Seaforth, and John, Lord Reay, dated at Achmore in Assynt, 4th July, 1672 (*Book of Mackay*, 439-440).

Once when the family at Bragar was short of meal, John Morrison left home in the morning to buy some, but in the evening returned with empty sacks, for he had unloaded what he had got at a little distance from the house. When his wife saw the empty sacks she began to scold him angrily. Morrison allowed her to go on till she was tired, and then went and fetched the meal. As soon as she saw it her mood changed, and she began to smile. John Morrison then said:—

Ni thu ghàire 'nair a gheibh thu min;
'S mist do ghean' bhi gun bhiadh;
'S b'fear leam féin na'n t-each dearg
Nach tigidh fearg ort riamh.

Translation.

You laugh when you get meal;
Your good humour is the worse for being without food;
I would rather than the red horse
That anger came not on you ever:

meaning that he would give his red horse to have her always in good humour.

To his various other talents John Morrison of Bragar seems to have added that of engineer; for Seaforth having—about 1660—undertaken the siege of the castle of Ardvrack, belonging to Macleod of Assynt, and finding he made but little progress, sent for John Morrison, who, having gone over the ground, recommended that four hundred raw cow-hides should be made into bags and stuffed with moss. The bags were placed in line and raised to the height of a man, and from the shelter of this rampart the besiegers fired upon their assailants without receiving any damage themselves. Some say the Mackenzies placed the wives of the Macleods upon the top of the rampart; at any rate the castle was quickly surrendered.[2]

John Morrison had five sons, four of whom, Roderick, Angus, John, and Murdo, seems to have inherited their father's genius; the fifth is said to have been Malcolm, who was appointed to the Chapel of Poolewe.[3]

[1] These epigrams of the Tacksman of Bragar are from the Rev. M. Macphail, Kilmartin, and the late Mr John Morrison, surveyor.

[2] Morrison's "Traditions of Lewis."

[3] Mackenzie's "Beauties of Gaelic Poetry," p. 85.

Roderick, called *An Clasair Dall*, or the Blind Harper, finds a place in Mackenzie's "Beauties of Gaelic Poetry;" but I have nothing to add to what is there stated, except that his father declared that he was put to more expense and trouble in bringing up one son as a muscian, than he would have had in educating three as clergymen.[1]

The fame of Angus, minister of Contin, occupies a wide space in folk-lore. He was "the last Episcopal minister of Contin, of whom many interesting anecdotes are still related, illustrative of his wit and benevolence. This excellent man suffered very harsh treatment for refusing to conform to Presbytery. He was rudely ejected from his own church, to which he had fled as to a sanctuary."[2] The writer goes on to say that he closed a long, honourable, and a useful life in great indigence; but I think this must be a mistake, for, besides that he owned the small property at Doire-na-Muic, by Little Loch Broom, we find that "Mrs Morrison, daughter of Mr Angus Morrison, the last Episcopal minister of Contin," left a legacy of £80, for charitable purposes, to the poor of Fodderty;[3] and that "Mrs St Clair, who died at Jamaica [possibly the same lady as the Mrs Morrison named above], a native of this parish [Contin], daughter of Mrs Æneas Morrison, minister of Contin," left a legacy of £100 to the poor of that parish.[4] He was living on his own property at Doire-na-Muic, by Little Loch Broom, in 1823, and travelled to Edinburgh in that or the following year.

The Rev. Angus Morrison, otherwise call Black Angus, was noted for his sagacity, wit, and good fellowship, as well as for being a learned and eloquent preacher. The *sgeulachdan* of the "Fathers of Ross-shire" are valuable, not so much for their historic truth, but as illustrating the way of life and mode of thought of that time. Alexander Mackenzie of Applecross and Highfield bought and sold cattle, and sometimes went with his drovers to England, where he sold them to great advantage. At one time, Mackenzie having sold his drove, was staying at a gentleman's house in Yorkshire, and, on the Sabbath-day, attended divine service. The preacher was a talented man, and much esteemed for his doctrine and eloquence. Conversation turning upon the discourse, Mackenzie said that there was a preacher in Ross-shire who excelled any they could bring against him in soundness of doctrine, fluency of speech, and clear and powerful delivery; and that he would stake £50 upon it. His English friend accepted the wager. When Mackenzie came home he went to Contin, and told Mr Angus of the wager. He replied, "Well, Sandy, I'll go with you to Yorkshire; but I fear you will have a poor chance for your money." Mr Angus let his beard grow, and for a snuff-mull he took a rough, undressed ram's horn of most uncouth appearance, and for a lid closed it with a pickle of straw. Applecross and Mr Angus arrived safely on a Saturday night at their destination, and on the next day, as the wager was well known, there was a large assemblage to hear the Scotch minister. It was then the custom, when rivals had to preach, that a text, from which they had to preach extempore, was placed in the pulpit by the Presbytery.

This story given verbatim from the MS in TGSI, XXXI. 364-5.

When Mr Angus entered the pulpit he was meanly dressed, and, with his long beard, presented an uncouth appearance. He looked round the pulpit for the slip of paper with the text upon it, and finding none, sat down, pulled out his ram's horn and took a pinch. At last one of the ministers got up, and asked him if he was going to address them. Mr Angus said they had given him no text. One of the ministers told him he could take his own beard and snuff-box for a text. I omit the sermon. Of course, Aaron's beard and its anointing, and what it was typical of, were introduced. In the evening the ram's horn was the text, which was illustrated by Joshua and his trumpets, with suitable applications and inferences. When the sermons were concluded, all the ministers gave their verdict in his favour. So Applecross won his wager, which he presented to Mr Angus, who had no scruple in accepting it.[5]

Other reminiscences would lead to the conclusion that the days of the Fathers of Ross-shire were not all so miserable as has been supposed; but they are passed over to give place to an instance of the sagacity of the minister of Contin. Some sheep had been stolen from a parishoner, and the soldiers at Fort-Augustus were suspected of the theft. With the consent of the commanding officer the soldiers were drawn up, when Mr Angus gave to each of them a straw, and told them he should know which of them was the thief, for he would be in possession of the longest straw. The man who was guilty of the theft shortened his straw to avoid detection, and was thereby discovered.

Mr Angus was as courageous as he was witty; for, having business in Edinburgh, he had arrived at Inverness, where he was informed that a desperate robber, of whom a party of soldiers was in pursuit, and for whom a reward was offered, was supposed to be lurking upon the road. Mr Angus, however, proceeded upon his journey, but was again warned that the robber had lately been seen in that neighbourhood. Mr Angus having a fast horse thought he might venture to proceed; but as he was passing through a wood the robber sprang from behind a tree, and, presenting a pistol at Mr Angus' breast, demanded his purse. Mr Angus, saying that his purse contained very little money, and that he would

[1] He may have been recorded in one of the two last volumes of Morrison's "Traditions of Lewis."

[2] N. S. A., Ross-shire, p. 237.

[3] O. S. A., vol. vii. p. 414; N. S. A., Ross-shire, p. 259.

[4] O. S. A., vol. vii. p. 166; N. S. A., Ross-shire, p. 243.

[5] Morrison's "Traditions of Lewis."

This story given verbatim from the MS. — TGSI, XXXI. 565.

× For his receipt for an Irish Bible see TGSI, XXXI. 344.

rather part with it than his life, told the robber to hold his horse; and, as the horse was very young and skittish, to take hold of the bridle with both hands. Mr Angus had a stout stick, and when he saw both hands of the robber engaged, he turned to one side, and instead of taking out his purse as the robber expected, he raised his stick and brought it down with such force across the arms of the robber as completely to disable him. Mr Angus then tied him to the tail of his horse, and returned to Inverness, where he received the reward for the capture and the hearty congratulations of the people.[1]

Of Mr Angus it is said, "his satirical wit was the terror of many in those days, so that any person who invited such a man to a treat, made the best shift he could to please him, and to part with him on good terms." When Mr Angus was living at Little Loch Broom, a neighbour pressingly invited Mr Angus to visit him, which Mr Angus prepared to do rather unexpectedly. The neighbour caught sight of Mr Angus coming towards his house, and not being, as he thought, sufficiently prepared to entertain him, he went into his house and told his wife to say that he had gone from home, and that he would not be back for two days. When Mr Angus entered, the mistress said what her husband desired her. But Mr Angus, who had his suspicions, told her that he would wait till her husband came back. The mistress was very uneasy all day, and towards evening brought a man, with a very large creel, into the *culaist*[2] or small room at the end of the house in which her husband was secreted. Mr Angus watched the mistress and the man with some interest, and presently saw the man returning with a heavy load upon his back. Mr Angus guessed what was in the creel, and, having his pocket-knife ready, he dexterously cut the strap of the creel as the man was passing the hearth. Both the creel and its contents fell into the fire, and the goodman roared for help. None was more ready than Mr Angus to render assistance, and to ask the goodman what could have induced him to practise such an expedient. The goodman made a clean breast of it, and added, that had he got out of the house, he would have come in as from a journey, and made the minister welcome to what he had. Mr Angus explained that he would have been contented with a herring and potatoes, and recommended a straightforward line of conduct in future.[3]

Another of the sons of the tacksman of Bragar was the Rev. John Morrison, sometime minister of Urray, in Ross-shire. On the 7th April 1719, the Rev. John Morrison of Urray, ordained and admitted the Rev. John MacGillegen of Altness, minister of Loch Ailsh.[4] I have stated before, that I suppose the Rev. John Morrison of Urray was the "Indweller," who wrote an account of Lewis, now in the Macfarlane Topographical Collections.[5]

The minister of Urray had a son, also called John, who was missionary at Amulree in 1745; he was settled in Petty, in Inverness-shire, in 1759, and in 1774 his successor was appointed. He was called the *Bard*, and one of his popular Gaelic songs was to the lady whom he had baptized, and to whom he was afterwards married.[6] According to Lewis tradition, he was chosen minister of Petty in a competition with four other candidates.[7] He was a highly-gifted and orthodox preacher, and was believed to be gifted with the spirit of prophecy in a wonderful manner.

The following tale illustrates some of the customs which I have seen in my youth. Mr John had a family of sons and daughters, and an orphan girl, Kate, was brought up with them. After some years Mrs Morrison died, and Kate had charge of the household. At last it was whispered about that Kate had been indiscreet, and an elder informed Mr John of the suspicion. The minister seemed to excuse Kate; said that human nature was fallible, and a great deal more which it would be irreverent in me to quote. The elder admitted that all his Reverence had said was quite orthodox, but asked permission to summon Kate before the Kirk-Session to be questioned.

The first day Kate was called before the session, and asked who was her paramour. She said she did not know his name, and that he was a drover. The elders became clamorous and threatening, in order to extort a confessions; but the girl would only give the same answer. At last Mr John interposed; he said he was more grieved than any of them for her folly; but that she ought not to be treated so harshly, and that her crime should not debar her from his protection and sympathy if her future behaviour evinced a sincere repentance. The members of Session could not tell why the minister should be displeased at their endeavour to force a confession, and they therefore began to suspect the minister himself. The first Sunday after the Kirk-Session one of the parishioners who had been incontinent was ordered to stand up, and the Kirk-officer was directed to put the sack-cloth over his shoulders; but the man made so much resistance that Mr John cried out to leave him alone till next Sunday, when he would have a companion. Everybody in the church wondered who this would be.

Early next week one of the elders, being at market, heard it said that Mr John was the delinquent, and went to tell him so. "Ah! well," said Mr John, "half a word from the Judge's mouth at the day of judgment

[1] Morrison's "Traditions of Lewis."

[2] *Culaist* is an abreviation of Cul-na-glais, behind the lock. Where the house is divided by two partitions into the three chambers, the inner one is the *culaist*.

[3] Morrison's "Traditions of Lewis."

[4] N. S. A., Ross-shire, p. 408.

[5] "Spottiswoode Mis.," vol. ii. p. 335.

[6] N. S. A., Rosshire, p. 409.

[7] But compare N. S. A., Rosshire, p. 410.

will clear me of that charge." The elder would rather that his Reverence might be cleared in this life.

On the next night Kate knocked at the window of a certain married man; she said there was of no use in her screening him any longer, for that he himself must have told the minister of their acquaintance. The man said that he had done nothing of that sort. "Then who could have told him," said Kate; "it will be well for you to go where he is to-morrow and own your guilt, and thereby you may come off the easier."

On the following Sunday the man was sack-clothed along with the other delinquent, as Mr John had predicted in the hearing of the whole congregation.[1]

The youngest son of John Morrison of Bragar was Murdo, and he was bred to be a smith.[2] He was a man of uncommon strength, and possessed a full share of the genius of the family; he could make swords and guns, though in a measure self-taught. He proposed at one time to his father to make a gun for killing deer. His father, doubting his ability, persuaded him not to attempt it. However, he set about it, and on a day he was fixing the gun into the stock when his father entered the smithy. His father said, "You have made a gun contrary to my advice, and I daresay it will never kill a beast." Murdo replied, "Do not judge prematurely, for I am just going to put a shot into it." There happened to be a lot of Mr Morrison's cows grazing at some distance from the smithy, and Murdo said, "What should I have to pay if I shoot that speckled ox from here?" "Well," said his father, "if you kill six of my cattle at that distance you will not have to pay a penny for the loss." Murdo fired at the stot, which fell, and Mundo told his father to send a servant to bleed the beast. John Morrison advised his son, if he wanted to keep so good a gun for himself, that he should put no ornament on it, nor fix it in the stock, but simply tie it on with cord, so that the ugly mounting should scare any gentleman from desiring to possess it. From this circumstance it was called *Gun na Sraing, i.e.*, the Rope Gun. In spite of its ugly mounting, Murdo did great execution in the deer-forest, and on one occasion, when returning from a visit to his brothers at Cotin and Urray, he arrived at Gairloch when there was a shooting-match for a silver cup. Each competitor had to put a half-crown into the cup, and Donald Roy Mackenzie, otherwise Donald Roy Mac Vic Urchy, formerly tacksman of Park, Lewis, and *co-alt* (fosterer or foster-brother) of Murdo, persuaded him to try. Murdo aimed at the target, and won both the cup and the money. The laird of Gairloch was so much pleased with Murdo that he sent him in his barge to Lewis.[3]

In those days Seaforth used to go once a year round Lewis to sport, when he would remain for a night at Mr Morrison's house at Bragar. On one occasion Seaforth had Mackenzie of Assynt with him and the captain of a man-of-war. Seaforth desired a peck measure to be brought, for he had been told that if a sword was properly tempered, it might be bent into the circle of the measure. The gentlemen took their swords, and all stood the trial but Seaforth's, which broke. Seaforth was somewhat disappointed with the result.

In due time the guests went to their beds, when John Morrison told his son that he must not go to his bed, but to his smithy, and try to mend Seaforth's sword. So father and son set to work, and when Murdo had mended and polished the sword, he handed it over to his father, and desired him to tell where it had been broken. His father could not see where it had been joined. Murdo then wanted to go to bed, but his father said, "Not yet; let us try if the sword will go into the peck measure without breaking." It did so. The half-peck was then brought, and it stood even that trial.

After breakfast next day, when Seaforth and his suite were preparing to leave, Seaforth put on the scabbard with, as he thought, the broken sword, muttering some words about breaking it. John Morrison then said that even here, in Bragar, the sword could be repaired and made better than ever. "Well," said Seaforth, "if you could get my sword mended and tempered so as to stand the proper trial, I would give you this year's rent of Bragar down." John Morrison replied, "Let us see the pieces and be thinking about it." Seaforth drew forth his sword, and, looking at it with astonishment, he remarked, that though he had passed the night in bed, that they, the Morrisons, had not taken their wonted rest.

The *Gun na Sraing*, although an ugly piece of furniture, was a very profitable one; but after Murdo Morrison's death, his son, Donald Morrison, who was tacksman of Harbost, at Ness, broke it in a fit of anger, and repented of his rash deed when there was no remedy.[4]

The Rev. Norman Morrison, grandson of John Morrison of Bragar, succeeded the Rev. John Macleod, who was the first Presbyterian minister of Uig. On 9th May 1763, the Rev. N. Morrison received a letter at Balnakil, Uig, dated 30th March last, from Macleod of Hamar (Theophilus Insulanus),[5] in Skye. In answer, the Rev. N. Morrison states that he

[1] Morrison's "Traditions of Lewis."

[2] The social status of a smith must not be compared with that of a farrier at the present day; besides his farm, his *cain* or dues gave him a competent livelihood. In the earliest time he made his own iron (in Sweden, certainly) which he fashioned into anything that was needed—needles, fishhooks, arms, armour, &c.; he manufactured the gold and silver ornaments of the wealthy, and was both jeweller and goldsmith.

[3] Morrison's "Traditions of Lewis."

[4] Morrison's "Traditions of Lewis."

[5] Carruthers "Boswell's Jour." p. 127.

× Probably William Dubh (VII), whose sister was mother of John Garbh Maclean I of Coll (*Macleods*, 14), and whose father John MacLeod VI died in Pabbay (*ibid.*). Killed at Bloody Bay 1480. Witness to charter in 1449.

will subscribe for a bound copy of Hamar's "Treatise on the Second Sight,[1]" then about to be published; but he assures Macleod that not one in his parish can read but himself.[2] The book might have been more useful to Mr Morrison had it contained instructions for dispelling these supernatural illusions; however, a demon having got into communication with Malcolm Macleod, tenant of Cliff, he applied to the minister, who gave him a written paper which he was to offer to the demon. When they next met, Malcolm presented the paper (the demon being the able to read, while Malcolm could not); but the demon was disgusted and, on Malcolm continuing to prosecute him with it, he disappeared and was never seen again.

But more unruly than the evil spirits were the spirits of some of his parishioners; for one of them, Donald Macaulay, tacksman of Brenish, having taken offence at the minister, locked him out of his own church; but the misdemenour was compromised by a fine to the poor's-box.[3]

About 1778 the Rev. Norman Morrison was succeeded in Uig by the Rev. Hugh Monro.

The Morrison clan, besides forming a large proportion of the population of Lewis, are numerous in Harris, North and South Uist, and Edderachyllis. The numbers of a clan-name is a good indication of the length of time that the clan has been settled upon the land. Often, by the irony of fate, the poorest beggar is the representative of the most ancient lord of the soil.

The Harris Morrisons claim to be of the original stock, and the following tradition concerning them is interesting.

Sometime in the fifteenth century, Macleod of Harris, who was a young man, was in Pabbay. He heard that Peter Morrison, a tenant in Pabbay, was an expert wrestler, so he collected the young men of the island and desired them to show their skill. So they began to wrestle, and Peter Morrison proved himself to be the best man. The laird then requested Peter to try a fall with himself; but Peter declined, for he said his temper was such that he could not yield to any man unless he was overpowered. Macleod commended him for his courage, and bade him act as he had said. They then grappled, and Peter soon laid Macleod upon his back. Macleod took no offence, but one who was standing by, thinking to gain the laird's goodwill, drew his sword and killed Peter. But when Macleod saw Peter fall he ordered his men to seize the murderer, who fled, but being closely pursued he jumped headlong over a precipice into the sea.

Peter Morrison left one son, and the kind laird brought him up with his own children, and as he displayed considerable ability he had the chief management of Macleod's estate.

Young Morrison was a comely person, and, in the suite of Macleod, visited Maclean of Coll. It was soon agreed between the chiefs that Morrison should marry one of Coll's daughters, but when he was called before them he modestly declined, as he had not wherewith to support a family. But the worthy Macleod said he had plenty to maintain them, and that the Laird of Coll would not see his daughter want. Then they went to the young lady's room, and asked her if she objected to marry Macleod's secretary and the chief manager of his affairs.

× See also *Dàin Iain Ghobha*, xvii.

× Calls him Donald in the *Traditions of the MacAulays*

The young lady discreetly answered that she could not refuse what had been arranged for her by her kind friends, but she requested of Macleod that, if she had sons, one should be a minister (priest) and another a smith; that Macleod should present the minister to a parish, and the smith the usual revenue belonging to his office. This was granted, and there was one son a priest in Harris, who the people remember as *A' Person*, and another son was the smith there. From this Morrison the smiths in Harris are descended;[1] and I add that while I write the smith in Harris is still a Morrison, and that Peter is yet a distinctive name in that family.

The following legends are of little historic value, but they often unconsciously record the ideas and customs of a remote age, and are eminently suggestive on that account. These legends, along with most of the ~~most of the~~ foregoing tales, have been selected either from the MS. "Traditions of Lewis," written by Mr John Morrison, cooper, Stornoway; or from the Rev. M. Macphail's "Traditions of Ness," which were obligingly collected by him in answer to my request for information concerning the "brieve of Lewis." He says that "most of them were taken down from the dictation of Angus Gunn, at North Dell, who not unfre-

[1] This work is a curiosity, and supplies much interesting matter. Hamar was strongly anti-Jacobite. The tradition concerning him is: Roderick Macleod, tacksman of Hamar, was a true patriot and a loyal subject. After the battle of Sherifmuir he was appointed by the Commissioners to uplift the rents of the forfeited estates in Skye and Uist, but managed his business, as king's factor, with prudence and compassion.

Hamar was travelling to Inverness with the king's rent, and had but one servant with him who was very strong, but not very wise. Hamar was surprised by three robbers as he was resting in a wood, and his servant was sleeping a little distance off. Resistance was useless, so he gave up the money. The robbers returned a crown to Hamar to pay his lodgings for a day and a night; but he declined it, and said he would be obliged to them if they would give a good slap to wake up his lazy servant. The robbers treated the kilted Highlander very rudely, but he sprang up so suddenly that he wrested a gun from one of them in a moment, and killed them both. The third fled; but Hamar, who had by this time got his gun, brought him down. By the clever stratagem of getting the violent temper of his man aroused he regained all his money. After this adventure Hamar always got some soldiers to be a guard when he was going to Inverness with money.

[2] "There are none but myself in the parish to use the book.—*Second Sight*, p. 161.

[3] Morrison's "Traditions of Lewis."

[4] Morrison's "Traditions of Lewis."

[illegible]. } Killed by Neil MacLeod 1597–1606.
[illegible], } (Ex. [illegible], 270–1)

Malcolm's. Gille-calum Mór, [illegible] [illegible]
by Norman, grandfather of Torquil Dubh ([illegible]),
Domnall, [illegible] 1213.

[illegible]. On [illegible] 1599 (WI, 194).

Son hanged in [illegible] for [illegible]
in [illegible] of Macleods in [illegible]
[illegible] ([illegible], 48) c.1560]
Murdo (see p. 34 n).

[illegible] of [illegible] [illegible] [illegible] (cf. HP II, 273)?

quently told the same story with additions and omissions; he died about a year ago." Gunn could not read and had no dates, but recited volumes of what he supposed to be the history of Lewis.

IAN BRITHEAMH, THE JUDGE OF LEWIS.

John Morrison was married twice; by his first wife, who was an Irish lady, he had four sons—Allan, Kenneth, Angus, and Murdo.[1] He used to go every alternate year for wood to Ullapool, where, after the death of his Irish spouse, he became enamoured of the only daughter of the tacksman of Ullapool (*aon nighean Fir Ullapoll*). The lady was not willing to accept him, but by the persuasions of the islander and her aged father she was induced to consent, and they were married.

When the marriage was over, *agus a charaid òg chur air leabadh*, and all the household were asleep, some one entered the bedroom of the wedded pair, and placed his hands upon them both. The brieve awoke, and demanded in a loud voice, "Who is this, and what do you want?" when the person, whoever it was, left the room without saying a word. But the bride began to cry, for she knew it was her handsome young lover, for whose sake she had at first refused the brieve. Next day the newly married pair sailed for Lewis; a daughter was born to them before the brieve made his voyage to Ullapool again, where, after taking in a cargo of wood, himself and crew slept in the boat, waiting the return of the tide. But during the night a blow with a club killed the brieve as he lay asleep, and the foul assassin escaped unseen. Before the Lewis men left on the morning, a fair-haired, handsome young man came to the boat, and seemed much distressed when he was told of what had happened. When they were about to leave, he said he had long been anxious to visit Lewis, and if they would give him a passage, and bad weather came on, that he would show himself to be as good a hand at the helm as their deceased master. He embarked with them, and took the helm all the way till they arrived at Ness.

As soon as they landed, the stranger asked a boy to show him the way to *Tigh mor Thabost*, *i.e.*, the Big House of Habost. The boatmen were astonished, and asked him how he came to know about the Hall of Habost. "I know something," said he, "about Habost." The stranger went to the house, and the brieve's wife welcomed her former lover. She asked him about her husband. "He is coming," was the answer. Presently the crew came up from the boat, and told her all that had happened, and that her husband had been murdered. The lady did not seem to take it much to heart, for her husband was hardly buried before she was again married, and to her first lover.

Allan, the eldest of the brieve's children, having arrived to sixteen years of age, claimed his father's sword and the right to use it. For such pretension his stepfather sought to kill him; but Allan fled to his mother's friends in Ireland. In the course of a few years they came back with him to assist him to get a share of his father's property. It was Christmas Eve when they landed at Ness, and as they came near the house they heard the sound of music, by which they knew that the inmates were enjoying a feast and making merry with their friends. Allan, embittered by the remembrance of the injuries he had suffered at their hands, was with difficulty restrained from rushing in and dealing with them in the midst of their merriment. But his uncles reasoned with him on the barbarity and cowardliness of so doing, and told him they would shed no blood without warning them of their danger, so that they might prepare for defence.

⊗ Làmh mo chridhe-sa làmh Eòin
Nach suidh an tigh an òil ghann,
Dh'fhuadaich e 'm Britheamh gu cladh,
Beul on tigeadh an lagh cum.

× Not so. Angus Bane McDonachie vc Ion vc Houston who died before 1662 was married to Catherine Morison sister of John Morison of Bragar, and left an only lawful son Rorie (Commissariot of the Isles.) cf. GN IV ..

Allan went into the kitchen and there saw his father's bard, neglected and despised, lying upon straw upon the the floor. The bard, on seeing his master's son, swooned with joy; the sight recalled to him the days when Ian *Cóir*[2] Britheamh was his patron, when on Christmas he used to be, not in the kitchen, but in the hall, and there the life and soul of the company. When the bard recovered his senses, Allan urged him to go to the hall-door and charge *him* with the murder of his patron, and not to fear, as Allan's party would be quite near to render assistance.

When the new bard saw the old bard at the door, he addressed him as follows :—

Fàilt' ort féin a bhàird Eòin,
Shuidh'riamh an tigh an òl ghann;
Dh' fhuadaich thu'am Britheamh gu chladh,
Am beul o'n tigidh an Lagh cam.

Translation.

Welcome to thee, oh ! bard of John.
Thou didst always sit where drinking was scanty.
Thou didst drive the Judge to his grave.
The mouth from which proceeded the crooked law.

Upon which the lady clapped her sides with delight. The old bard, finding his worthy master and himself insulted in this manner, denounced his mistress in the following reply :—

A bhean bhaoth, 's a bhean bhaoth,
Teann a nall ach ei do bhreith
Fuath do'n fhear do'n rug thu clann
'S gràdh do'n fhear thug'cheann dheth.

[1] Murdo is a mistake for Donald, and Malcolm Mor is forgotten.
[2] *Cóir*, Gae., just, upright, good, hospitable.

p. 12 [illegible]

⊗ J.S.A. account – HP II. 213.

× Angus (GN VIII. 83, 92)

Cf. *An Gàidheal*, (1876), p. 47 ff.

* and [illegible] [illegible] Beng. (Edition) [illegible]

§ Kenneth and ~~[illegible]~~ Donald.

Translation.

Oh wicked woman, oh wicked woman,
Draw nigh that we may know your opinion.
Hatred to him to whom you bore children,
And love to the man that beheaded him.

The party, quickly understanding the reason of the old bard's boldness, fled from the house and escaped to the mainland. Allan Morrison regained his heritage, and became Brieve of Lewis.[1]

No corroboration has been found of this obscure tale. The events belong to a period anterior to the sixteenth century. That the widow of a brieve married the murderer of her husband is supported by the tradition that John Macleod of Sandey did so. Of course, there is no truth as concerning him, and the event may have been borrowed from a tragedy that was enacted on an island in Loch Stack, Edderachyllis. Sir Hugh Macky of Far fell desperately in love with a beautiful woman, who resisted his addresses on the score that she had a husband. The miscreant detained the wife upon the island, caused her husband to be murdered, had the corpse decapitated, and produced his head to the wife. The widow offered no more opposition, as she feared a like fate for herself.[2] Sir R. Gordon's account is that Y. Macky slew Tormat-Mack-can-Woyr (Mhór) [Macleod], the chieftain of that race, violated his wife, and had a son by her, called Donald-Balloch-Macky.[3]

[1] Rev. M. Macphail's "Traditions of Ness," MS.
[2] O.S.A., vol. vi. p. 294.
[3] Sir R. Gordon's "Earl of Sutherland," pp. 136, 307.

Allan Mòr Morrison, Judge of Lewis.

Many a wild and impossible story has been invented from the shadowy remembrance of the tragedies of the seventeenth century, of which the following is an instance :—

Neil Macleod, called in the legend *Odhar, i.e.*, dun, the bastard uncle of Torquil Duth Chief of Lewis, attacked the Morrisons on the Habost moor, but was defeated. Neil sent to Harris for assistance, and came again to Habost; but the Morrisons had taken shelter in Dun Eystein. The Macleods arrived at night and marched to Dun Eystein, when one of the Morrisons, unaware of the presence of an enemy, came out of the hut. An Uig man shot an arrow—*Baobhan Dòrlaich*, literally, the Fury of the Quiver, the last arrow of the eighteen that should be used—at him, and he was struck by the arrow, which passed through his body. The wounded Morrison cried for help; the rest came out, and Allan, the eldest, and by far the bravest, of them sprang across the ravine which separated Dun Eystein from the adjacent cliff, and loudly demanded that the assassin should be given up to him. The Macleods denied all knowledge of the deed; but Allan reproached them with cowardice, and said, "If you have come to fight you ought, according to the laws of war from the creation of the world, to have waited till there was light enough to see each other." He then asked Neil for his *Leigh, i.e.*, Doctor, to attend the wounded man. Neil, after some hesitation, consented; Allan took the *Leigh* under his arm and leaped back across the ravine with him into the dun. The wounded man died, however. The Morrisons fled from Dun Eystein to the mainland, whither Neil pursued; but the Morrisons had seen Neill crossing the Minch, and, slipping out from among the islands, tried to get back to Lewis. The Macleods ascended a hill, espied the briev's birlin, and gave chase. There were only Allan Morrison and his two brothers in the boat; so Allan Mor, who was very strong, set his two brothers to row against himself, and composed and sung this *iorram* or boat song, with which the Ness fishermen still lighten their toil.

The chorus "*Nàilibh i 's na-ho-ro*," is repeated after every line :—

Cf other versions in *An Gàidheal* (1876), 49; *Eilean Fraoich*, 30; *Carmichael* *MSS*. No. 115.

Iomair a Choinnaich fhir mo chridhe ;
Iomar i gu làidair righinn ;
Gaol nam ban òg's gràdh nighean.

Dh' iomrain fèin fear mu dhithis,
'S nam éiginn e fear mu thri.
Tha eagal mòr air mo chridhe
Gur i biorlinn Neill tha' tighinn,
No eathair Mhic Thormaid Idhir.

'S truagh nach robh mi fèin 's Nial Odhar
An' lagan beag os ceann Dhun Othail ;
Biodag nam laimh, is e bhi fodham,—
Dhearbhinn fèinn gun teidheadh i domhain ;
'S gun biodh fuil a chlèibh 'na ghabhail.

Translation.

CHORUS.—" Na liv ee, 's na-hò-rò ; " words having no meaning.

Row, Kenneth, man of my heart ;
Row with vehment might ;
The darling of damsels, and the beloved of girls.

I myself could row against two ;
And may be against three.
There is great fear on my heart
That it is Neill's barge that is coming,
Or the boat of the son of dun Thormod.

× cf. *An Gaedheal* (1876), 49.

It is a pity that I and dun Neil were not
In a small hollow above Dun Oo-ail;
A dirk in my hand and he beneath.
I would be sure it should go deep,
And that the blood of his breast should flow down his feins.

Neil overtook the Morrisons a short time after they had passed Dun Othail (pro. Dun Oo-ail), where they fought desparately. Neil attacked them on one side, and the Harris men, in a second boat, on the other. Allan engaged Neil's party and killed nearly all his men, when Neil exclaimed, "My men, something must be done, or the monster (*biaft*) will not leave a head on the shoulders of any one of us." They fastened a sword to the end of an oar, therewith to stab Allan, who, when he saw it coming, made such a desperate blow as to cut the oar in two, but striking into the gunnel of the boat his sword stuck fast, and before he could extricate it the Macleods closed round him, and both himself and his two brothers were killed. They were buried in a small hollow a little above Othail.[1]

In this story we have the distinctly Scandinavian notion that it was wrong to slay after dark. Among the Northmen, and no doubt among all other peoples in the same barbarous stage, the mere killing of a man was of little importance,—in Burnt Njol, the atonement for a foul assassination was only twelve ounces of silver,—but it was murder if the killing was done at night; *nátt-vígg eru morð-víg*, "Is it not called murder to kill people at night?" So, too, Sweyn, Earl Hakson's son, objects to captives being killed, because "it was night." "Burnt Njol," vol. ii. p. 26.

With regard to the *Léigh* (Læknir, Icel.), Leech or Surgeon, it might be supposed that the bard had imported a foreign idea into his tale. Though I have found no record, yet it may be inferred that a chief would be attended by his hereditary doctor in time of war. But there is no reason why the Macleods and Morrisons should have ever been in want of a doctor; for so late as 1793 the natives of Edderachyllis were nearly all of the names of Macleay, Morrison, and Macleod. These Macleays were the descendants of "Ferchard Leche," *i.e*, Ferchard Beathadh, Beaton or Bethune, a native of Islay, and who was physician to King Robert II. In 1379 "Ferchard, the king's physician," had a grant of the lands of Mellenes and two parts of Hope, in Sutherland ("Or. Pr." vol. ii. part 2, p. 704); and in 1386 "Ferchard Leche" has a gift of all the islands near the coast between the Stour in Assynt and Armadale, Sutherland (*ib.* p. 695). The Clan Beaton or MacBeathadh were a medical clan, and there are notices of them in Islay, Mull, South Uist, and Far in Sutherland. One of them, the "famous *Doctor* Beaton," of Mull, had the dubious fortune of being blown up when on board the Spanish ship Florida, in Tobermorry, but escaped unhurt (Martin's "West. Isles," p. 254).

It was a cold and snowy day when, under the guidance of the shepherd, by wading through overflowing brooks and wet heather, I reached the cliff above Dun Othail, which rose before me desolate and grand "through storm and rock," and at any time is one of the most picturesque objects in Lewis.

Dun Othail is a natural fortress, being an irregular peaked rock, upon the sea coast, nearly 200 feet high, and disjoined from the main by a perpendicular ravine which, however, does not reach to the water. The sides of the ravine appear to have been the walls of a trap-dyke, which has been denuded. The dun is only accessible from the land on the south-east side, and there it is defended by a wall. I was unable, through fatigue, to proceed beyond this, but the Rev. M. Macphail informs me that, although there is no defensive masonry upon the rock, it is so difficult of access that the path which leads upwards could be defended by a single individual.

An oblong ruin upon its extreme point is supposed by Mr T. S. Muir to have been a chapel.[2]

Dun Othail is famous in Lewis legends; the ubiquitous *Coinneach Odhair* (Kenneth Oear) has prophesied that there will be great destruction of the Lewis people by sword; but—

Amhainn Lacsdail fo thuath,
Ag an Cuinnich am mòr shluagh;
* * *
Ach thig a mach a Dun Othail
Na bheir cobhair dhoibh 's fuasgladh.[3]

That is:—

At the North Laxdale river,
Where the great multitude of people will gather;
* * *
But one shall come out of Dun O-ail
That shall render them help and relief.

The deep ravine dividing Dun Othail from the main is called *Leum Mhac Nicol, i.e.*, Nicholson's Leap; and it is made to be the scene of a legend of which I have several and various editions. One of them may

[1] Rev. M. M'Phail's "Traditions of Ness," MS.

[2] "Characteristics of Old Church Arch," pp. 2, 162.

[3] This prophecy is not in the interesting collection made by Alex. Mackenzie of the "Propheicies of the Bracan Seer," Inverness, 1877.

× John MacLeod (Iain *Borb*), 6th Chief; 1370 – c1442 (*MacLeods*, 12)

be briefly told as follows:—MacNicol, for some misconduct, was sentenced by the chief of Lewis to be mutilated. In revenge he ran away with the only child of the chief, and, being pursued, he leapt over the chasm to Dun Othail with the child in his arms. Persuasion was used to induce him to surrender the child; but he refused unless the chief were reduced to the same condition as himself. Several subterfuges—which are too technical to be repeated here—were tried to deceive MacNicol, but in vain; and to save the child the chief consented. When MacNicol was sure that he had gained his purpose, he sprang with the child over the cliff into the sea, saying (in Gaelic of course), "I shall have no heir, and he shall have no heir."

Now, this tale is a good instance that where the accidents of a place are fit, a legend is either originated there or is transferred to it. The South Uist people claim the scene of this tragedy to have been at Huishness, South Uist; and "Nicholson's Leap" is marked on Johnston's map. Nearly the same tale is told of a place in Mull, and probably elsewhere. But the original tragedy occurred a long way south of Lewis; according to Gerald Barry it was "*apud castellum Radulphi*," at Chateau Rouse, now the chief town in the department of the Indre, in France. The story is told in the "Itinerary through Wales," chap. xi., in words of the same meaning as those used by the bards of Lewis at the present day. It is most singular that an event which happened so far away, and probably more than seven centuries ago, should, though falsely located, be told in the islands with such distinctness. Whether it has been passed on from mouth to mouth, or whether it has been read from Giraldus by intelligent priests, it is nearly certain that it has been kept alive by repetition for at least three or four hundred years.[1]

[1] Roll's Edition, p. 84.

] 550

Allan Morrison and the Demon.

Macleod of Lewis possessed Assynt and Cogach (but not Strath Connon, only his son was married there); and when he was passing some time in those countries, he left the sole management of Lewis to Judge Morrison of Ness. Donald Cam and Neil Macleod being dead, the sons of the Judge ruled the country most tyrannically.

Allan Morrison, the Judge's eldest son, was intimate with a demon; this coming to the ears of Macleod of Lewis, Allan was sent for by him, and was asked if it was true; Allan confessed it was. Macleod then said, "The next time you meet the demon, ask whether I shall die a natural death or not." Allan returned in a few days, and said that the demon foretold that the present Laird of the Lewis would be killed by a Macleod then living. But the wicked Allan Morrison feigned this story, for the demon had said that either Allan or his father would be killed by the hands of a John Macleod.

In consequence of this information, Macleod of Lewis left the country for his other estates, for he did not consider himself safe while a single John Macleod was left alive in Lewis; and Judge Morrison obtained his sanction to bring all the Macleods in the country before his court as suspected persons.

Judge Morrison now began the trial of the suspected Macleods. He killed sixteen of the Macleods of the name of John, for it was by a John Macleod that Judge Morrison was to lose his life. But after he had disposed of all the John Macleods in this manner, the demon or spirit told him that it was by John Macleod of Harris, that he or his son was to be killed.

The Judge had then recourse to conspiracy, and engaged sixteen stout and able men to swear to support him in his bloody plot. He sent one of his men with a letter to the Laird of Harris, saying, that as the Judge had now the sole management of Lewis, he sent him his respects, and requested Macleod to meet him on a certain day to sport and hunt deer in the hills of Lewis. John Macleod of Harris had been by this time forewarned of Judge Morrison's plot, so he answered, that having been lately sporting in the Lewis hills, he would rather that the Judge should come to sport with him in Harris.

The Judge and his sixteen warriors arrived at Rowdle, and were hospitably entertained by Macleod for the greater part of the night. But while the Judge was enjoying himself, quite happy in the thought that he would take Macleod's life upon the hills on the next day, Macleod gathered his chief men about the house; suddenly a strong body of swordsmen entered the hall, and bound Judge Morrison and his sixteen warriors. The Laird of Harris now produced the letter which a friend in Lewis had written, telling about the conspiracy. Macleod offered pardon to the sixteen men, who had been forced to join the plot, provided they would return peaceably to Lewis, which they joyfully accepted. The Judge was hanged at Rowdle; and thus the prediction was fulfilled in spite of the shifts made to avert it by the bloody massacre of the Macleods in Lewis.[1]

This myth has besn elaborated, from the facts that John Macleod of Sanda killed Ian Breitheamh, *i.e.*, John the Judge, defeated Malcolm Mòr, his son, and carried him to Stornoway, where he was beheaded.

CAIN MORRISON.

Judge Morrison, who was executed at Rowdle, was succeeded by his

[1] Morrison's "Traditions of Lewis."

son-in-law, Cain Morrison, in the office of Judge. This Cain Morrison was originally a Macdonald, born in Ardnamurchin. It appears the proprietor of that estate exacted his right to pass the first night with every bride. A vessel had come to anchor in the loch on the day that Cain had married. Cain did not rest at all on the night on which he was married, but wandered about much grieved. In the morning he was met by the captain of the ship, to whom he spoke of the evil practice of that country. The captain said that that vile custom ought to be done away with, and that he would lend him his cloak and sword. "Watch about the Laird's house, and when he comes out, look intently up to the castle, and say that you see a serious crack in the wall. Have your sword ready inside your cloak, and when the Laird looks up, have at his throat and kill him. Then run to my boat, which shall be in waiting, and I will carry you to where you shall be safe." Cain acted on this advice, and escaped with the shipmaster, who landed him at Ness, where he married a daughter of Judge Morrison, and succeeded to his office.[1]

Mercheta mulierum was a fine paid to a lord by a vassal on the marriage of his daughter; for if she married a *villein* on another barony, the lord, being deprived of part of his *live-stock*, required indemnification for the loss. But *Mercheta mulierum* was, in later times associated in idea with *jus primae noctis*, with which, as Lord Hales shows, it had no concern. The foregoing legend illustrates the vulgar notion of *Mercheta mulierum;* and I well remember that the then proprietor of Cava, in the Orkneys, was assured that he had such privilege in that island. The Lords of the Isles are said to have exercised such right; but this, from the nature of the case, is absurd. It is unnecessary to go further into the subject here; but if the following extract from a history of the Macdonalds has any foundation in fact, it shows that a state of manners existed in the Highlands so late as between 1506 and 1510, as would justify the most extreme views that have been held concerning *Mercheta mulierum.*

"During the time that Archibald [Gillespick Dubh of Sleit] kept company with these outlaws, Angus Collach, his brother, went with a great train to Uist, and as the custom then was, he must needs have for his partner that night the goodman's daughter, or in case of his having no daughter, he must have his own wife. He came to St Mary's, the principal church of North Uist, nigh to which Macdonald of Belranald lived, a gentleman descended of Godfrey, who had to his wife a daughter of John Brainish, son of Allan, the son of Roderick of Muidort, who had Benbecula for his patrimony. This gentleman, Donald Macdonald, being in the meantime absent from home, his wife went to church to hear mass, and Angus Collach, meeting her at the church, and saluting her, told her he meant to lodge with her next night, to which she made him welcome. He observed that she must herself partake of a share of his bed. She replied, when he came to the house she would give him an answer. So Angus went to her house next night, and was received by her very kindly, upon this he began to urge her earnestly to perform her promise. She replied, that it was not yet bedtime, and when it was she would be his partner for the night. So before she ordered supper to be brought to them, she got a horse ready to the house, and while he and his retinue were at supper, she rides under night to Benbecula, where her father was."—*Hist. of the Macdonalds, Knock MS.*

Macleod of Lewis, having found out that he had been imposed upon by Allan Morrison, returned to Stornoway Castle. He settled Torquil, his son, at Strath Chonen; his youngest son was sent to Cain Morrison's house at Ness; and a son of Cain Morrison was fostered by Macleod at Stornoway, thus showing the friendship and good understanding between the families.

When matters had continued in this way for some time, a wicked man who used to be going back and fore between Ness and Stornoway, came one day into Macleod's castle and said that Cain Morrison had, in a violent passion, killed Macleod's child. Macleod unfortunately believed it to be true, and in his anger killed the son of Cain Morrison. The wicked incendiary then flies off to Ness, and tells that he saw Macleod kill the young Morrison. Cain, on hearing of the murder, could not conceive any reason for it, and though the young Macleod was much loved by all the family, he was not spared.

Thus the peace of those families was broken by this wicked incendiary. It is told that when Judge Morrison, with the laird's concurrence, executed all the John Macleods in Lewis, some of the relations of this wicked man suffered with them, and this was the way he took to revenge the death of his friends; and it was through him that the Macleods of Lewis became extinct. Instead of peace between the Macleods and Morrisons, there was now nothing but murder and bloodshed. Cain Morrison was at last obliged to flee to the mainland, where he was killed by a cottar in an island by Loch Broom, since then called "Judge's Island."

Allan More Morrison then took his father's place at Ness, and fighting

[1] Morrison's "Traditions of Lewis." Norman Macleod, "the Bard," has nearly the same story; but the account of "Kain Morrison," noted by the Rev. M. Macphail, turns on a different subject.

went on between the two clans whereby both suffered severely in their property and friends.[2]

The circumstance which gave name to *Eilean a' Britheimh*, or Judge's Island, has been described above. The custom of sending a child to be fostered in a family which had been at deadly feud with the parents of the child, although intended to strengthen in the strongest manner the truce between the families, often led to his destruction. We shall have another instance of fosterage in the murderer's family in the traditions of the Lewis Macaulays.

In an edition of the Letterfearn MS. History of the Mackenzies, copied into Morrison's "Traditions of Lewis," after stating that the brieve was hated for his treachery to Torquil Du, there occurs, "as also killing a son of M'Leod's [~~Torquil Du's~~] when a child nursing in his own house." This sentence is not in Gregory's copy of the Letterfearn MS., but it is the only corroboration I can find of the preceding legend.

The Four Torquils.

Soon after Cain Morrison was killed at Loch Broom, the Laird of Macleod himself died. He had three [legitimate] sons, who were each named Torquil, viz., Torquil the Heir, Torquil Connonach, and Torquil Du; he had also another son named Torquil Ogg. They all died before their father, and the cause of their deaths was as follows:—

Macleod the Laird was married four different times. The first wife died and left a son called Torquil the Heir. The second wife had a son whom his father also named Torquil, and his wicked mother bribed some mainland men to hang the heir at Ullapool, that her own son might succeed; he was called Torquil Connonach. The second wife died; the laird married a third time, and had a son named Torquil Du (who had a son named John), and his mother employed wicked hands to kill Torquil Connonach at Sandwick [by Stornoway]. The third wife died, and the laird having married again, the fourth wife found means to have Torquil Du shot upon the moor by a couple of bloody men, named Mac Mhurchy, a branch of the Macphails or Mackenzies.

Macleod was now old and sickly, but coming to know that his wife had caused the murder of Torquil Du, he told his wife to send up their infant child, Torquil Ogg, or Young Torquil, that he might know by manual operation whether the child was fit to be his heir. The child was taken to his father's bed, when he handled the boy's body, and, in revenge of his mother's doings, he squeezed his sides together and so killed him. He then told his mother that the child would not stand the trial necessary to constitute him his heir, and that he was dead. And he added, "As you, bad woman, have left me without an heir, so I have left you without a son." He then expired.[3]

There is no historic truth in this legend, but it shows to how late a period the power of the father over the fate of his child was supposed to exist. According to Dascent, among the pagan Northmen, "as soon as a child was born it was laid upon the bare ground; and until the father came and looked at at, heard and saw that it was strong in lung and limb, he lifted it in his arms, and handed it over to the women to be reared, its fate hung in the balance, and life or death depended on the sentence of its father."—Burnt Njol, vol. i. p. xxv.

"On the introduction of Christianity into Iceland, A.D. 1000, it was resolved that, in regard to eating of horse-flesh and exposure of children, the old laws should remain in force; as Grimm remarks, the exposure must take place immediately after birth, before the child had tasted food of any kind whatever, and before it was besprinkled with water (*au sa vatni*) or shown to the father, who had to fix its name; exposure after any of these acts was murder. The Christian Jus. Eccl. put an end to this heathen barbarism by stating at its very beginning, *ala skal barn hvert er borit verdr*, *i.e.*, all children, if not of monstrous shape, shall be brought up" (Cleasby's Icelandic Dic., p. 58; cf. Conybeare's "Place of Iceland," &c., p. 147.

The practice of giving the same name to two brothers is still common in the islands.

How the Morrisons got Rona.

The possession of the island of Rona was a subject of dispute between the Morrisons and the people of Sutherland. The mainland people claimed it, because, as they asserted, the island lay nearer to Sutherland than to Ness. At last it was agreed that the contending parties should race for it, and that the island should belong to those who first lit a fire there. On the day of trial the mainlanders seemed likely to be the first to reach to, and make a fire upon the island; but a Morrison shot a burning arrow from his boat and set the grass on fire, and Rona has belonged to Lewis ever since.[4]

[2] Morrison's "Traditions of Lewis."

[3] Morrison's "Traditions of Lewis."

[4] Rev. M. Macphail's "Traditions of Ness." In Morrison's "Traditions of Lewis" it is Macleod of Harris and Macdonald of Slait who race for St Kilda. Two boats were to be built of equal size, they were then to cast lots for them, and whoever got first "and kinded a fire therein," was to possess the island. "In this way Macleod of Harris became proprietor of St Kilda originally."

One of the customs of the Northmen, by which they took possession of, or as they called it, hallowed, land to themselves, was by raising a fire upon it. It seems to have been sufficient to have lit a fire at the mouth of a river to constitute a claim to all the land through which that river flowed. But what more immediately bears upon the preceding legend is told in the settlement of Iceland:—"A man, who was called Onund the Fore-knowing (*virs*), took up land from Merkigil and all the valley eastward of it; and when Erik [an adjacent landnamman] thought of taking the west end of the valley, Onund fell to divination (*felldi blotspan*) to make him prescient (*virs*) of the time when Erik intended to come to take the valley; but then Onund was the quicker [of the two], and shot a burning arrow (*tund-ör*, tinder-arrow) over the river, and so appropriated or hallowed (*helgadi*) to himself all the land westward, and [he] dwelt by the river." Land., p. 193; Cleasby's Dic., p. 254.

With these legends we close the "Traditions of the Morrisons." Although the authorities have been carefully consulted, it is probable that a native of Lewis could have greatly extended them, and perhaps have found something to repress; but a comparative stranger has the advantage of being able to tell the whole truth,—a liberty seldom enjoyed by a family historian.

www.ingramcontent.com/pod-product-compliance
Lightning Source LLC
Chambersburg PA
CBHW021418090426
42742CB00009B/1177

* 9 7 8 3 3 3 7 3 8 9 4 2 0 *